THE KINGDOM OF AGARTTHA

A JOURNEY INTO THE HOLLOW EARTH

—◆—

MARQUIS ALEXANDRE SAINT-YVES D'ALVEYDRE

TRANSLATED BY JON E. GRAHAM

Inner Traditions
Rochester, Vermont

Inner Traditions
One Park Street
Rochester, Vermont 05767
www.InnerTraditions.com

Originally published in 1886 in French under the title *Mission de l'Inde en Europe* by
 Calmann Lévy, Éditeur, Paris
First U.S. edition published in 2008 by Inner Traditions

Library of Congress Cataloging-in-Publication Data

Saint-Yves d'Alveydre, Joseph Alexandre, marquis, 1842–1909.
 [Mission de l'Inde en Europe, mission de l'Europe en Asie. English]
 The kingdom of Agarttha : a journey into the hollow earth / Marquis Alexandre Saint-
Yves d'Alveydre ; translated by Jon E. Graham. — 1st U.S. ed.
     p. cm.
 Includes bibliographical references and index.
 ISBN 978-1-59477-268-9 (pbk.)
 1. Occultism. 2. Earth—Internal structure—Miscellanea. I. Title.
 BF1999.S31213 2008
 130—dc22

                                                                    2008023293

Printed and bound in the United States

11

Text design by Diana April
Text layout by Virginia Scott Bowman
This book was typeset in Garamond Premiere Pro with Gill Sans as the display typeface

Contents

Alexandre Saint-Yves d'Alveydre

INTRODUCTION

SAINT-YVES D'ALVEYDRE AND THE AGARTTHIAN CONNECTION

———

Joscelyn Godwin

In 1884 the French occultist Saint-Yves d'Alveydre (1842–1909)[1] decided to take lessons in Sanskrit. Having just published his definitive work on the secret history of the world, called *Mission des Juifs* ("Mission of the Jews"),[2] he was anxious to deepen his understanding of the sacred languages, which, he felt sure, concealed the ultimate Mysteries. Hebrew had already revealed much to him; now it was time to tackle the even more ancient language of Sanskrit, parent of all the Indo-European tongues.

Saint-Yves' Sanskrit teacher came to him through a mutual friend, General Dumont.[3] Calling himself Hardjji Scharipf, he was a character of hazy origins and the subject of various rumors. Born on December 25, 1838, he supposedly left India after the Revolt of the Sepoys (also called the Indian Mutiny) of 1857 and set up in the French port of Le Havre as a bird-seller and professor of Oriental languages.[4] His name may have been a pseudonym; he may have been an Afghan; some called him Prince.[5] In short, much rumor and speculation have surrounded him, and most writers on Saint-Yves have not taken him very seriously.

One reason may be the only published photograph,[6] which, as one of them says, makes him look like someone got up as a Turk for a fancy-dress ball.[7] But this is an underestimation. The manuscripts for which Hardjji was responsible, now in the Library of the Sorbonne in Paris, show that he was a learned and punctilious teacher, and the source of two still unsolved enigmas: the holy land of Agarttha, and its sacred language of Vattanian.

In 1882 Hardjji had written out an elaborate Sanskrit grammar, presumably for some earlier student, which he gave to Saint-Yves.[8] He wrote it in beautiful script and in French, with notes that show some command of English, Hebrew, and Arabic. Sometimes he added explanations that he signed with his initials "H. S." One of these, for instance, was on the mortuary customs of the Hindus. Here and there he inserted criticisms of foreign Sanskritists, particularly British ones, who thought that they understood the language perfectly. At one point he quotes a passage from the Laws of Manu that mentions a great deluge, and remarks on how foolish it is to take the Hindu and Hebrew Flood legends literally.

Hardjji lived in a northern suburb of Paris, Levallois-Perret; Saint-Yves, in a much more fashionable quarter, in a private house on Rue Vernet near the Place de l'Étoile, to which he had moved after his fortunate marriage in 1877. Their Sanskrit lessons began on June 8, 1885, and continued three times a week for at least a year and a half.[9] Saint-Yves's wife, Marie-Victoire, a very independent and cultured lady, joined in at least the earlier lessons.[10] Each day, Hardjji would carefully write out a lesson of grammar and a reading from some Sanskrit classic such as the Laws of Manu, or, toward the end of the course, the Bhagavad Gita. In the corner of every page, as in his grammar of 1882, he signed his monogram. Though I do not know Sanskrit, I am impressed by the methodical work and the progress that Saint-Yves made under Hardjji's tutelage.

Mystery enters the picture in the heading of the very first lesson:

*First Lesson in the Sanskrit Language
to Monsieur the Marquis Saint-Yves d'Alveydre
Paris, this 8th of June 1885 [Hindu dates follow]
by Teacher and Professor H. S. Bagwandass
of the Great Agartthian School*[11]

Saint-Yves must have asked him what this "Great Agartthian School" was, and received an answer, though perhaps not as full an answer as he would have liked. He might already have read in the books of the popular travel writer and historian Louis Jacolliot[12] of an "Asgartha," supposedly a great city of the ancient Indian priest-kings, the "Brahmatras." Does such a place still exist, then? Apparently Saint-Yves was given to believe so, and, what is more, that it preserves a language and a script, known as "Vattan" or "Vattanian," that are the primordial ones of mankind. For someone in quest of the secret and sacred roots of language, the mention of such things must have been unbearably exciting.

Curiosity overcame him on Christmas Day, 1885. The day's lesson was the beginning of the Bhagavad Gita, on which Hardjji had noted the date of its context: "51,900 (the confusion of languages, etc.)." Conversation on the confusion of tongues must have led to the subject of humanity's previous language. Might Saint-Yves learn it now? If not, perhaps Hardjji would at least be good enough to spell his pupil's name in Vattanian characters? The guru obliged, writing it on the back of the lesson sheet and adding wryly: "Here, according to your ardent desire; but really you are not yet sufficiently prepared for Vattan. Slowly and surely!"[13] Later he must have taught Saint-Yves the Vattanian alphabet and the principles behind its letterforms, which Saint-Yves would correlate with the Hebrew alphabet and with the zodiacal and planetary symbols. On the back of the lesson for January 13, 1886, there is a caption: "Model of Vattanian elements for the Agartthian rite alone, for the use of initiates."[14] Perhaps the elements were delivered at the same time, on a separate sheet.

Saint-Yves' admirer Papus would write, with characteristic overstatement though well within his master's lifetime, that the latter "was initiated into the tradition of the Orient by two of the greatest dignitaries of the Brahmanic Church, of whom one was the Brahatma of the holy centers of India. Like all the pupils of the true Oriental initiation, he possessed all the teaching notebooks, of which every page is countersigned by the Brahmin responsible for the transmission of the holy word."[15] One of these notebooks survives.[16] It is rich in entries in Hardjji's handwriting and in Agartthian references. There are several informal conversations written out in Sanskrit with word-by-word French translations, including the following significant phrases: "Our guru Hajji Shariph Bagwandas by name, of the town of Bombay of cardinal Agarttha in India," and ". . . how was he able to leave Agarttha?"[17]

On another page is written "The first divine Agartthian journal," and on the last page, Hardjji has penciled a prayer with some Vattanian symbols: "Master of the Universe and Protector of the holy land Agarttha, in the name of the . . . grant me, who am thine and whose thoughts are upon thee and in thee, the . . . of thy sublime goodness, as a Yogi twice-born in soul and body; from which vow I will never depart. Om Sat tat, Brahma Visnu Civa isan tê Ha-hi-Ho-Hva avoh!"[18]

By the time this notebook was being compiled, Agarttha and Vattanian had evidently become subjects for study and conversation. But this is a sketchy and disorganized notebook, mostly written in pencil, marking the transition of Saint-Yves' interests from pure Sanskrit to a kind of comparative Hermeticism. The core and the key to this synthesis appear in a much grander manuscript written in red and gold ink, and using all four of Saint-Yves' distinct handwritings. It contains invocations, sigils, many alphabets, designs, and arabesques made from Sanskrit and Vattanian letters; a list of Vedic and Biblical names encoded in a so-called Hermetic or Raphaelic Alphabet;[19] eighty "Vedic" symbols representing the development of the cosmos;[20] a passage on the "Hermetic Significance of the Zodiac" encoded in planet and zodiac signs; correlations of these signs with the names of angels and with

Vattanian, Sanskrit, Hebrew, and Hermetic characters; breathing exercises for the hearing of the inner sound "M" and for soul-travel;[21] notes on the properties of herbs; and alchemical recipes.

It is interesting that Hardjji signs all these pages with his monogram, even the ones purely derived from Western esotericism. But he seems to have progressively lost interest, his signature becoming sketchier until it is no more than a little cross. Then, in the middle of a section on "Botanical Magic," it disappears for good. Was it from this point that Saint-Yves was left to his own devices?[22]

With or without Hardjji's cooperation, Saint-Yves seems to have been searching for a way to relate Western Hermeticism of the Renaissance type, with its emphasis on alchemy, Christian Kabbalah, and magical correspondences, to Hindu cosmogony and metaphysics as expressed in the primordial symbols of Vattanian. But his methods were practical as well as theoretical. At one point, early in his marriage, it is fairly certain that he experimented with laboratory alchemy.[23]

He also practiced clairvoyance (or perhaps, on this occasion, employed a medium), for he encodes in Vattanian characters the following psychic warning: "Beware in eighteen months or two years of an assassination of my wife by a blond Russian in autumn. Stay occupied this autumn close to Marie. On Friday, June 17, 1887. Clairvoyance of *degio* [?]."[24] In fact, Marie-Victoire (who was Russian) lived till June 7, 1895, when she died at the age of 67. She then continued to manifest as Saint-Yves' "Angel" and to inspire his later work. In 1896 he returned to the Hermetic notebook, which he had laid aside ten years earlier, and, blessed by her continuing presence, filled it with further schemes and developments. These now bore the name of the "Archeometer," the universal system of knowledge on which he would work for another dozen years, leaving behind enough material for his disciples to compile imposing posthumous volumes.

But we must return to 1886, the year of Sanskrit lessons and Agartthian conversations. Did Hardjji know that Saint-Yves was writing another book—the present one—under the influence of his

Oriental studies? The book was finished, typeset, and printed by the same publisher (Calmann Lévy) as had issued Saint-Yves' *Mission des Souverains, Mission des Ouvriers,* and *Mission des Juifs.* To this series of "Missions" of sovereigns, workers, and Jews he now added the *Mission de l'Inde en Europe; Mission de l'Europe en Asie*: "Mission of India in Europe; Mission of Europe in Asia"—the original French title of the present volume.

To put it bluntly, this book takes the lid off Agarttha. The reader will learn that it is a hidden land somewhere in the East, beneath the surface of the earth, where a population of millions is ruled by a Sovereign Pontiff, the "Brâhatmah," and his two colleagues the "Mahatma" and the "Mahanga." This realm, Saint-Yves explains, was transferred underground and concealed from the surface-dwellers at the start of the Kali Yuga (the present dark age in the Hindu system of chronology), which he dates to about 3200 BCE. Agarttha has long enjoyed the benefits of a technology advanced far beyond our own, including gas lighting, railways, and air travel. Its government is the ideal one of "Synarchy," which the surface races have lost ever since the schism that broke the Universal Empire in the fourth millennium BCE, and which Moses, Jesus, and Saint-Yves strove to restore. (This was the theme of *Mission des Juifs.*) Now and then Agarttha sends emissaries to the upper world, of which it has a perfect knowledge. Not only the latest discoveries of modern man, but also the whole wisdom of the ages is enshrined in its libraries, engraved on stone in Vattanian characters. Among its secrets are those of the true relationship of body to soul, and the means to keep departed souls in communication with the living. When our world adopts Synarchic government, the time will be ripe for Agarttha to reveal itself, to our great spiritual and practical advantage. In order to speed this process, Saint-Yves includes in the book open letters to Queen Victoria, Emperor Alexander III of Russia, and Pope Leo III, inviting them to join in the great project. This was not quite as arrogant as it sounds, for he had a line to Queen Victoria through his friend the Earl of Lytton, and actually obtained her permission to dedicate a later work to her;[25] while through his wife, he was connected with the Russian aristocracy.

Perhaps the oddest thing about this book is Saint-Yves' own stance. Far from presenting himself as an authorized spokesman for Agarttha, he admits that he is a spy. Dedicating the book to the Sovereign Pontiff and signing it with his own name in Vattanian characters (just as Hardjji had written it out for him), he expatiates on how astounded this august dignitary will be to read the work, wondering how human eyes could have penetrated the innermost sanctuaries of his realm. Saint-Yves explains that he is a "spontaneous initiate," bound by no oath of secrecy, and that once the Brâhatmah gets over the shock, he will admit the wisdom of what Saint-Yves has dared to reveal.

How did Saint-Yves obtain this information? Already in his first book, *Clefs de l'Orient* (1877), he was writing with the confidence of an eyewitness of the psychic phenomena accompanying birth, death, and the relation between the sexes.[26] In the present work he seems to have extended his psychic vision, to say the least, and one can glean from here and there an idea of his methods.

There is, for instance, a passage here describing in detail how the Agartthian initiates travel in their souls while their bodies sleep (see page 77). Then there is the passage in the notebook already mentioned, on yogic exercises for separating the soul from the body. Thirdly, there is a snippet of occult gossip in a conversation with Saint-Yves recorded on August 16, 1896, by a psychical researcher, Alfred Erny:[27]

He has talked to Papus and [Stanislas de] Guaïta, but did not tell them what they wanted to know: the method of disengaging and reengaging oneself in the astral body. It is dangerous: "I don't want (he said) to put a loaded revolver into your hands which you don't know how to use."

"A magnetizer," he said, "runs less danger than others in duplicating himself, because he is more trained."

"When one goes out of one's body into the Astral, another evil spirit may replace you."

Saint-Yves presumably possessed the secret of this "somnambulistic" faculty, and used it to gather the information he presents in this book. But did he gather it, as he claims, from spying on a physical Agarttha beneath the surface of the earth? Or was it the result of his own projected fantasies or hallucinations? Or, again, did it come from some non-physical location or state which can be accessed under certain conditions, but which then merely supports the psyche's own subjective expectations and prejudices? We will return to these questions at the end.

I doubt that Hardjji Scharipf read the book, or had anything to do with its creation. From the manuscripts one can see that he did talk with Saint-Yves about an "Agarttha" and that he boasted a title from a "school" of that name that had "initiates" and "rites." But that is a far cry from the interpretations his pupil put on it. After all, there are people today who call themselves Rosicrucians, without necessarily believing that Christian Rosenkreutz lived from 1378–1484 and that his tomb still exists somewhere in Germany. Nor does a Buddhist of the Pure Land School situate the Western Paradise of Amitabha on the map of the world. Saint-Yves, on the contrary, was a literalist. *Mission de l'Inde* was not intended as an allegorical or symbolic work, on the lines of esoteric fantasies like the *Chemical Wedding of Christian Rosenkreutz*. He had no gift for fiction: all his other writing is deadly serious, and this one, however bizarre, is presented as a factual report.

No sooner was the book printed and ready for the bookshops than Saint-Yves withdrew it, destroying every copy but one. The work narrowly escaped oblivion, but this one copy passed after Saint-Yves' death to Papus, who published it in 1910, with some omissions, under the auspices of a group of disciples, the "Friends of Saint-Yves." Decades later, it turned out that the printer, Lahure, had secreted another copy.[28] The late Jean Saunier, biographer and chief authority on Saint-Yves, used this as the basis for the complete reedition of 1981, of which the present work is a translation.

Various reasons have been put forward for Saint-Yves' withdrawal of the book. Jules Bois, the occult gossipmonger, wrote unkindly that Saint-Yves' Brahmin teacher repudiated his pupil's "infantile mysticism," being disgusted by the "fantastic interpretations that this gracious but cracked brain gave to his lessons." Bois attributes to Saint-Yves the excuse that the said Brahmin had menaced him with the "dagger of the initiates" if he revealed these secrets, but says that in point of fact he merely threatened a lawsuit.[29] But Saunier discounts this on the grounds of Hardjji's cordial letter of December 24, 1887, which shows the two men still on excellent terms.[30]

I think that Saint-Yves, as he himself says in the book, had decided quite independently to publish his "researches" for the benefit of humanity, but that outside pressures forced a change of heart. For one thing, in July 1885, Victor Meunier had written a review showing that Saint-Yves' masterwork, *Mission des Juifs,* had plagiarized lavishly from the works of Fabre d'Olivet (1767–1825).[31] That was embarrassing enough, and Saint-Yves' excuses never really exonerated him. But there was worse to come. In 1886, Claire Vautier, a former opera singer, published a novel called *Monsieur le Marquis, histoire d'un prophète* (Monsieur the Marquis, History of a Prophet), in which Saint-Yves, transparently presented as "Saint-Emme," was given the most humiliating exposure as the lover who had seduced and abandoned her.[32] The book was all the more painful for being extremely close to the truth. Saunier, a most careful biographer, considers many of the character Saint-Emme's speeches as representing Saint-Yves' own experiences and philosophy. And one has only to glance through Vautier's other novels with their eloquent titles[33] to see that she could not possibly have invented his words herself.

In 1886, besides his Sanskrit studies and Agartthian visions, Saint-Yves' external and political activities on behalf of Synarchy were coming to a head with the formation of a Press Union (*Syndicat de la Presse économique et professionelle*), deputations to the President, etc.[34] After the embarrassments just mentioned, he cannot have wanted to risk the further mockery and ridicule that would have followed publication of a book that made such extravagant claims, and the harm it would have done to the more worldly wing of his campaign. And perhaps even he had been hurt too much.

The full public revelation of Agarttha was therefore withheld for the duration of Saint-Yves' lifetime, nor did he publish any significant doctrinal works after this point. But there is no doubt that he remained true to his vision. For instance, he mentions Agarttha and names its three rulers in his epic poem of 1890, *Jeanne d'Arc victorieuse*.[35] In his conversations with Erny in 1896, he stated outright that there exists a secret "Superior University" with a "High Priest" who is currently an Ethiopian, and other details just as they appear in this book. Finally, he mentions Agarttha in veiled terms in *L'Archéomètre,* the major work of his last years.

After the death of Marie-Victoire, Saint-Yves moved from Paris to an apartment near the Château of Versailles, where he installed a Catholic shrine to his wife. He continued till the end of his life to enjoy the status of *éminence grise* of French esotericism, sublimely aloof from the innumerable sects, cults, and quarrels of the time. Although he never belonged to any secret society, fraternity, or order (as far as we know), he was much revered by Papus, Stanislas de Guaïta, Charles Barlet, and other eminences of the occultist *fin de siècle.* Those whom he consented to receive left with impressive memories of his presence and conversations.

He was still there in 1908, when the young René Guénon (1886–1951) embarked on his esoteric career. Early in that year, certain members of Papus' Martinist Order (though certainly not Papus himself) had held a séance in which they were informed, through automatic writing, that they should form a new "Order of the Temple," and that twenty-one-year old Guénon should be its head. They continued with over forty table-rapping and automatic writing sessions. Saint-Yves' inspiration is evident from the start, when the subjects included "The Lost Word, the Origins of Language, the Vattanian Alphabet and its derivatives . . .

Archeometry and the origins of the Red Race," etc.[36] What is unclear is whether these were subjects suggested by the participants for clarification by the "spirits," or whether they arose spontaneously from the latter. In any case, Guénon emerged from these sessions with most of the themes of his future books already in hand: books such as *Man and His Becoming According to the Vedanta* (published 1925), *The Symbolism of the Cross* (1931), and *The Multiple States of the Being* (1932), which would give new meaning to metaphysics in the West.

Not long after, Guénon is said to have received Oriental doctrines by word of mouth, though his instructors have never been satisfactorily identified. The proof is there in his works: no young man since Pico della Mirandola had been in such confident possession of the highest metaphysical doctrines, which would provide the foundation for the Traditionalist or "Perennialist" school of spiritual philosophers.[37]

We may appear to have wandered far from the "Great Agartthian School" of Hardjji Scharipf. After the trauma of the First World War, the very name of Agarttha might have been forgotten, and Saint-Yves' book might have sunk out of sight like many an occultist's fantasy. But in 1922, a Polish self-styled scientist named Ferdinand Ossendowski published a sensational travel and adventure book.[38] It told of his flight through central Asia in the aftermath of the Russian Revolution. While in Mongolia, he heard tell of a subterranean realm of 800,000,000 inhabitants called "Agharti"; of its triple spiritual authority "Brahytma, the King of the World," "Mahytma," and "Mahynga"; of its sacred language, "Vattanan"; and many other things that corroborate Saint-Yves. The book ended on a dramatic note of prophecy from one of Ossendowski's informants: that in the year 2029, the people of "Aghardi" will issue forth from their caverns and appear on the surface of the earth. The prophecy was attributed to the King of the World when he appeared before the lamas in 1890. The King had then predicted that there would be fifty years of strife and misery, seventy-one years of happiness under three great kingdoms, then an eighteen-year war, before the appearance of the Agartthians.[39]

An unprejudiced reader, finding in three chapters of Ossendowski's book a virtual outline of Saint-Yves' Agarttha, not omitting the most improbable details, would conclude that the author had capped an already good story with a convenient piece of plagiarism, altering the spellings so as to make his version, if challenged, seem informed from an independent source. But Ossendowski denied this indignantly. When he was introduced to René Guénon, he said that if it were not for the evidence of the daily journal he had kept, and of certain objects he had brought back, he would have thought that he had dreamed parts of this story, adding: "I'd much prefer that!"[40]

Guénon's interest was rekindled, and in 1925 he wrote about the striking parallels between Ossendowski's Agharti and Saint-Yves' Agarttha:

> One can evidently debate the significance that should be attributed to all these similarities, but we do not think that they are sufficient to permit a conclusion unfavorable to M. Ossendowski. In any case, he has affirmed to us that he had never read Saint-Yves, whose name even was unknown to him before the French translation of his book; and for our part, we have no reason to doubt his sincerity.[41]

Two years later, Guénon published his most controversial book, *Le Roi du Monde* (The King [or Lord] of the World), in which he announced: "Independently of the evidence offered by Ossendowski, we know from other sources that stories of this kind are widely current in Mongolia and throughout Central Asia, and we can add that there is something similar in the traditions of most peoples."[42] Unfortunately Guénon does not support his claim to privileged access by telling us what these sources are, nor what degree of similitude is meant by "stories of this kind."

Near the end of *Le Roi du Monde,* Guénon faces the ontological question of whether Agarttha really exists:

Should its setting in a definite location now imply that this is literally so, or is it only a symbol, or is it both at the same time? The simple answer is that both geographical and historical facts possess a symbolic validity that in no way detracts from their being facts, but that actually, beyond the obvious reality, gives them a higher significance.[43]

So Guénon at the very least did not deny a geographical Agarttha. To his way of thinking, if one were found to exist beneath the surface of the earth, it would only corroborate the superior reality of the symbolic one. The Guénon expert Jean-Pierre Laurant comments on this that "the two interpretations have in fact nothing contradictory about them; they can even join with an appetite for the marvelous that Guénon never repudiated, his life long."[44]

Reading the present book and the last chapters of *Beasts, Men and Gods* side by side, one repeatedly finds passages that, occurring in vivid detail in Saint-Yves, recur in miniature in Ossendowski. These are often the most bizarre and absurd things, such as one might recall (unconsciously? we must give him the benefit of the doubt) from a book read years before. For example, there is a race of Agartthians with two tongues, with which they can speak different languages simultaneously. (Saint-Yves was fond of that one: he repeated it to Alfred Erny in 1896.) One cannot help wondering how Guénon and other defenders of Ossendowski would have reacted to such stories if they had been told by some Theosophist or Spiritualist. The matter is settled, to my mind, by Ossendowski's words on Sakhya-Muni (i.e., Gautama the Buddha), in a speech attributed to a Mongolian lama:

The blissful Sakkia Mounti found on the mountain top tablets of stone carrying words which he only understood in his old age and afterwards penetrated into the Kingdom of Agharti, from which he brought back crumbs of the sacred learning preserved in his memory.[45]

No Buddhist lama would have told such a tale, but a Hindu Brahmin might have, and Saint-Yves definitely does (see page 81), with the implication that where Buddha failed to garner the wisdom of the hidden kingdom, he has succeeded.

Ossendowski's account was later investigated by Marco Pallis, the traveler, writer on Buddhism, and translator of Guénon, with the advantage of his own contacts with highly-placed Indians, Tibetans, and Mongolians.[46] One of the latter, now very old, had been the head lama of a monastery at the time of Ossendowski's visit there. He testified that the latter's stories of the King of the World and of Agarttha bore no relation to any authentic legend or doctrine whatsoever, and that Ossendowski's command of the Mongolian language had not been nearly sufficient to understand what he claimed to have heard. Pallis's Hindu friends, similarly, disclaimed any Sanskrit source for Agarttha. The inevitable conclusion was that the credulous Guénon had been misled by Saint-Yves' fantasy, and that promoting belief in Agarttha in *Le Roi du Monde* had been a foolish mistake.

Certain believers in Guénon's infallibility, for whom Guénon himself had taken on the aspect of an emissary from the King of the World, were outraged by this.[47] In a more moderate vein, a "close collaborator of Guénon" who insisted on anonymity (Reyor again?) answered Pallis's conclusions in a letter to Jean Saunier by explaining that in 1927, as the result of the publication of *Le Roi du Monde,* there had resulted a rupture between Guénon and "certain of his Hindu informants." The writer points out that opinions differed in 1927 on the advisability of divulging information on the "secret realm," and asks why it should be any different today. "It would be normal—without this showing any disrespect whatever towards Mr. Pallis—that the Orientals interviewed by the latter did not feel obliged to confirm a divulgation which had not been unanimously approved."[48] In other words, the underground kingdom of Agarttha does exist as Guénon and Saint-Yves maintained, but it is no business of inquisitive Westerners.

Once Ossendowski's best seller had brought the Agarttha myth out of the esoteric closet, it began to enjoy a new lease on life. Others were quick to exploit it, such as a pair of adventurers who flitted through the Parisian scene in the late 1920s. Their version went as follows.[49] In the summer of 1908 (the same year as the refoundation of the Order of the Temple by Guénon and his friends), a young Franco-Italian, Mario Fille, met a hermit who lived in the hills near Rome. Going by the name of Father Julian, this hermit confided to Fille a sheaf of old parchments, telling him that they contained an Oracle. It worked through word and number manipulation, but the processes called for were painstaking and lengthy, and Fille did not bother with them until about twelve years later (i.e., about 1920), at a time of personal crisis. Thereupon he followed the instructions, which were to phrase one's question in Italian, adding one's name and the maiden name of one's mother, turn them into numbers, and perform certain mathematical operations with them. At the end of several hours' work, a final series of numbers emerges, which, when retranslated into letters, gives a cogent and grammatically correct answer to one's question. Fille was amazed. Apparently the Oracle never failed to behave with perfect reliability, though its answers were sometimes in English or German.

One of the first questions to ask such an oracle is of course "Who are you?" Fille, working with his friend Cesare Accomani, learned that this was called the "Oracle of Astral Energy"; that it was not a method of divination like some Kabbalistic oracles or the I Ching, but an actual channel of communication with the "Three Supreme Sages" or the "Little Lights of the Orient," who live in—Agarttha.

The Oracle's answers are elaborate, but not always conclusive, e.g.:

Q. "Do the Three Supreme Sages and Agarttha exist?"

A. "The Three Sages exist and are the Guardians of the Mysteries of Life and Death. After forty winters passed in penitence for sinful humanity and in sacrifices for suffering humanity, one may have special missions, which permit one to enter into the Garden, in preparation for the final selection, which opens the Gate of Agarttha."[50]

Fille and Accomani settled in Paris, where they demonstrated the

Oracle to a group of Orientalists, journalists, and writers, four of whom were impressed enough to write prefaces to Accomani's book about it. One of these was René Guénon, fresh from publishing *Le Roi du Monde*, but he withdrew his commendation before publication, having failed to receive "certain confirmations" of the Oracle's pronouncements.

One of the preface writers, the Tantric expert Jean Marquès-Rivière, quotes the opening of the *Emerald Tablet of Hermes*,[51] and writes that, in conformity with the Hermetic principle of correspondences:

> The center of transhuman power has a reflection on the earth; it is a constant tradition in Asia, and this Center (a terrestrial one? I DO NOT KNOW TO WHAT DEGREE) is called in central Asia *Agarttha*. It has many other different names, which there is no point in recalling here. This Center has as its mission, or rather as its reason for existence, the direction of the spiritual activities of the Earth.[52]

The following year, 1930, Marquès-Rivière published his own fantastic travelogue, *A l'ombre des monastères thibétains* ("In the shadow of Tibetan monasteries"), which culminates in an encounter with an unknown Adept who says that he is an envoy from the Kingdom of Life. "Our monastery is the immense Universe with the seven gates of gold; our Nation is above and beneath the earth; our Kingdom is in the three worlds of this cycle." The Adept adds that:

> In former times the center of the Master of the Three Worlds was not where it is now. There were times in this cycle when the Tradition of life was known and adored almost openly; the spiritual Center of the world was in the valley of a great river; then It moved, before the rising tides of the barbarians, towards the Orient, where It now resides, mysterious and hidden from the eyes of men.[53]

Marquès-Rivière's Adept does not name this Center. In the foreword to the book Maurice Magré refers to it not as Agarttha but by the well-known Tibetan name of Shambhala. There is no doubt that this group, now calling themselves the "Polaires," identified the one with the other.[54]

From now on, the true believers in Agarttha became indistinguishable from the popularizing writers who continue to exploit the myth for its sensational value.[55] However, even if one dismisses Guénon's Agarttha, Ossendowski's Agharti, and Saint-Yves' Agarttha as a mere literary transmission, it still leaves two independent sources: the books of Jacolliot and the manuscripts of Hardjji Scharipf. Louis Jacolliot (1837–1890) was for many years a magistrate in Chandernagor, South India, and collected numerous sacred texts and tales. His particular obsession was to prove that everything in European civilization has been borrowed from India, especially the legal system and the pagan and Christian religions. While he embellished what he was given and was irresponsible about citing his sources, it seems improbable that he altogether invented the account in *Le Fils de Dieu* (1873) of "Asgartha," the "City of the Sun," the seat of successive "Brahmatras" (spiritual and temporal sovereigns) for over 3000 years before its conquest by the Aryans about 10,000 years ago. (He gives as his source the Vedamaga.) As far as I can tell, this was the first appearance of our term in Europe.[56]

Hardjji Scharipf's manuscripts corroborate the Indian sources of Jacolliot. They show an Oriental from Bombay bringing to the West, in apparent sincerity, the notion of a "Holy Land of Agarttha" and its protector the "Master of the Universe" (who so resembles the "King of the World"). These manuscripts in the Library of the Sorbonne are in fact the sole piece of concrete evidence of an Eastern origin for the term Agarttha. Everything else known up to now has been mediated by a Western writer.

New light on Saint-Yves' Indian connections appeared in 1935. This came from Jean Reyor (pseudonym of Marcel Clavelle), who was an influential figure in the French esoteric world, an editor of the review *Études traditionnelles,* and a close associate of René Guénon. Reyor wrote that some Hindus, concerned to give to the West certain forgotten traditional doctrines, had fastened on Saint-Yves as one who, in his "Missions," had shown suitable tendencies. But since this project did not succeed as planned, he received only incomplete doctrines, and was finally judged unsuitable for the role and left to himself. Saint-Yves strove for the rest of his life, says Reyor, to make something of these incomplete doctrines, and his Archeometer was the result.[57]

Reyor gave some further details a few years later, in his preface to the 1948 edition of Saint-Yves' *Mission des Souverains, par l'un d'eux* (Mission of the Sovereigns, by One of Them, first published 1882):

> It seems that Saint-Yves entered into relations from 1885 onwards not with a Hindu but with an Afghan, "prince" Hardjij [*sic*] Scharipf, who doubtless had a large part in the composition of [the present book]. Later, at a date, which we cannot specify precisely, Saint-Yves was in contact with a Hindu, far more "serious" than Hardjij Scharipf, we believe, and who originated from North India. It was probably the information, albeit fragmentary, received from this source, that was at the origin of Saint-Yves' work on *L'Archéomètre,* a work, which, left in an embryonic state, was published in the volume carrying this title after the death of the author.[58]

Writers on Saint-Yves often refer to this second Indian, but without naming him. The only primary evidence I have found for him is in Saint-Yves' own analytic index to his notebooks. Here he lists one notebook as "Secret teaching of the Brahmins, communicated to me by the Rishi Bagwandas-Raji-Shrin."[59] Although the name seems to consist entirely of honorifics, it may be that of the "more serious" guru. Yet in the course of these notes, Saint-Yves also writes "Hardjji says . . ." The teachings in question connect some of the Vattanian symbols with theogonic, cosmogonic, and psychogonic events, amplified with Hebrew and Sanskrit root words.[60] They consist of only a few pages, without any monogram of Brahmanic approval such as Hardjji was wont to add. Saint-Yves would develop them at length in an essay, which exists in several careful manuscript drafts, eventually included in *L'Archéomètre* as "The Archeometer and Oriental Tradition."

Reyor's implication that these Oriental contacts were part of a deliberate action to introduce certain ideas to the West invites one to look for exactly what it was that might have attracted "them" to Saint-Yves in 1885. The general consensus is that it was *Mission des Juifs* in particular. Now, in the long preamble of that work, devoted to such topics as the Ages of the World and the advanced sciences of Antiquity, Saint-Yves suddenly breaks in to announce a new discovery he has made on January 3, 1884. It is a letter from what Saint-Yves calls "one of the affiliates of the great Fraternity of the Himalayas."[61] He gives a French translation of it, calling it a "pure Orient pearl" set in his chapter, and exclaiming that "Several thousand years ago, an initiate of the Ionian Mysteries could not have spoken better or more clearly if he had been present in thought at the actual spectacle of this world's events."

The letter in question deals with science, India, cycles, miracles, thought power, and a variety of other subjects. It is, in fact, one of the famous *Mahatma Letters,* written by the Mahatma Koot Hoomi, one of the Masters of the early Theosophical Society, to A. O. Hume, and published by Alfred Percy Sinnett in his first book, *The Occult World* (1881).[62]

Nine years before Saint-Yves' discovery of the letter, in 1875, Helena Petrovna Blavatsky and Henry Steele Olcott had founded the Theosophical Society in New York. In 1879 Madame Blavatsky and Colonel Olcott moved to India, where the Society came under the auspices of Mahatmas Koot Hoomi and Morya, residents of Shigatse in Tibet. This is not the place to discuss who or what the Mahatmas really were,[63] but they explained their patronage of the Theosophical Society as part of a seven-year experiment to see if the West was receptive to the wisdom the East had to offer.[64] They chose Hume and Sinnett for the experiment not as initiates but as ordinary Westerners. Hume soon fell out with them, but Sinnett, as a prominent Anglo-Indian newspaper editor, was excellently placed to publicize the Mahatmas' philosophy, which he did through *The Occult World* and *Esoteric Buddhism* (1883). However, the Mahatmas apparently became disillusioned, and their correspondence with Sinnett ceased.

To one way of seeing things, it was not by chance that in 1885, certain Hindus made contact with Saint-Yves, who had shown himself sympathetic to Oriental doctrines and whose career as a social prophet and publicist was on the rise. Once contacted, he was encouraged to learn Sanskrit, to read the Bhagavad Gita, and was given certain metaphysical teachings in an appropriately symbolic form (the signs of Vattanian). But we know the sequel: he was carried away on the one hand by magical correspondences, alphabets, codes, and all the apparatus of the Hermetic tradition; and on the other, by astral travel to fantastic realms.

Just as Sinnett never lost his modernist prejudices, thus disqualifying himself as a spokesman for Oriental tradition, so Saint-Yves never surrendered his conviction of the superiority of the Judeo-Christian religion. Although full of respect for the East, he would write in *L'Archéomètre* that it would eventually be necessary for India to be converted to a "Christian and Catholic Order," with Sanskrit as its liturgical language.[65] In Jean Reyor's words, "It seems that Westerners, even when they manifest traditional tendencies, cannot resign themselves to not being superior to the rest of the world. One can believe that such an attitude contributed not a little to preventing Saint-Yves from profiting fully from the Oriental teachings, which he had occasion to receive."[66]

In other words, the Eastern sages tried using him, as they had used Sinnett, to lift a corner of the veil concealing their secrets, and then dropped him. The admirers of René Guénon may have cause to believe that with a third attempt, they succeeded.

It is time to summarize, and to draw whatever conclusions are possible in this enigmatic business. First, we have two independent witnesses to an Indian Agarttha tradition. Louis Jacolliot was led to place it in the past, as the ancient Brahmanic capital. For Hardjji Scharipf it was a living initiatic school with its own secret script. Until a reputable scholar comes forward with data on the myth of Agarttha, and especially on the Vattanian alphabet,[67] my working hypothesis is that they were part of a mythology belonging to a restricted and obscure Indian school, which has only surfaced to Western notice on these two occasions.

However, Saint-Yves wanted more than the tantalizing taste that his Sanskrit teacher allowed him. He therefore decided to use his gift for astral travel to explore Agarttha further, and was rewarded by visions of an underground utopia and its Sovereign Pontiff, the spiritual Lord of the World. What is the source, and the ontological status, of such visions?

There are, one gathers, definite places or complexes in the Astral World (also known as the "Inner Planes" of magic), which present to the clairvoyant visitor certain invariable features. I have heard reliable reports, for instance, that libraries are to be found there, in which the initiate is able to further his philosophical study while his body rests. But the incidental circumstances of such a place vary, according to the visitor's own cultural conditioning and expectations. Some find themselves, for example, in what they believe to be the Alexandrian Library, or in Atlantis, i.e., a place of the past. To others, it seems current and contemporary, though preferably in an inaccessible location like the Himalayas. The décor is a trivial matter, of course, in comparison to the philosophical truths to be discovered there, but the glamour of it sometimes overwhelms the traveler. Then his attention fixates on irrelevant details, and an inflated sense of self-importance may result. Thus Saint-Yves, convinced that he has penetrated to the realm of the world's spiritual ruler, writes about four-eyed tortoises, two-tongued men, levitating yogis, and ends up addressing pompous letters to the Queen, Emperor, and Pope.

I can accept that in some state of altered consciousness he saw what he claims to have seen. But like many who habitually indulge in altered states, he was not able to situate either his visions, or himself as witness to them, with the requisite philosophical detachment. The result is a classic case of misplaced concretism.

Yet there is a grandeur to this book. Its vivid and elegant prose lifts it far above the logorrheic authors of visionary and channeled literature (e.g., Emanuel Swedenborg, Anne Catherine Emmerich, Andrew Jackson Davis, *Oahspe*, or the *Urantia Book*). In sheer weirdness of imagination it rivals the fantasy fiction of Lovecraft or Borges, while in deadpan seriousness and titanic self-confidence it compares to prophetic works like the Book of Ezekiel or the various Apocalypses. And it reminds us that the earth is a very strange place, with many unexplored corners, many enigmas, and many surprises in store for us surface-dwellers.

Joscelyn Godwin, musicologist and historian of ideas, teaches at Colgate University. He has written widely on the Western esoteric tradition, concentrating on France and the 19th century. He is the translator of the 1499 architectural-erotic novel *Hypnerotomachia Poliphili*. Godwin's books include *Harmonies of Heaven and Earth*, *Music and the Occult*, *Arktos: The Polar Myth*, *The Theosophical Enlightenment*, *The Pagan Dream of the Renaissance*, *The Real Rule of Four*, and *Athanasius Kircher's Theatre of the World*.

NOTES

1. See my article, "Saint-Yves d'Alveydre and the Agarthian Connection," *The Hermetic Journal* 32 (1986): 24–34; 33 (1987): 31–38, on which this introduction is partly based. Further on Agarttha and the related but very different myth of Shambhala, see my *Arktos: The Polar Myth in Science, Symbolism, and Nazi Survival* (Grand Rapids: Phanes Press/London: Thames & Hudson, 1993; reissued Kempton, Ill.: Adventures Unlimited Press, 1996), 79–104. Further on Saint-Yves, see my *Music and the Occult: French Musical Philosophies, 1750–1950* (Rochester, N.Y.: University of Rochester Press, 1995), 181–96.

2. Saint-Yves d'Alveydre, *Mission des Juifs* (Paris: Calmann Lévy, 1884; reprinted Paris: Editions Traditionnelles, 1971, 2 vols.).

3. See the transcription of General Dumont's letter to Hardjji on the bottom of page 161.

4. For Hardjji's birth date and address, see the facsimile of his letter to Saint-Yves

reproduced here, on pages 162–63. The other details appear in Jules Bois, *Le Monde invisible* (Paris: Flammarion, 1902), 37–38.

5. See the statement of the "Amis de Saint-Yves" on the top of page 161.

6. See the portrait of Hardjji Scharipf on page 158.

7. Marco Pallis, "Les sources d'Ossendowsky," *Sophia Perennis* (Tehran) 2, no. 2 (1976): 72–89; reprinted in symposium *René Guénon* (Paris: L'Age d'Homme, 1984), 145–54, and as "Ossendowski's Sources," *Studies in Comparative Religion* 15, no. 1/2 (1983): 30–41.

8. This, together with Saint-Yves' Sanskrit lessons, is in the Bibliothèque de la Sorbonne, Nouveau fonds de manuscrits, Ms. Carton no. 42. Saint-Yves, who had no children of his own, left his manuscripts and books to his step-children, Count and Countess Keller, who passed them on to the famous French occultist Papus (Dr. Gérard Encausse). Papus's son, Dr. Philippe Encausse, gave them to the Sorbonne in 1938.

9. There are forty-one numbered lessons, mostly undated but with names of the days in French and English, beginning June 8, 1885, then regularly dated every Monday, Wednesday, and Friday from Dec. 9, 1885, to Feb. 10, 1886, and from June 14 to Nov. 12, 1886.

10. For reasons of space, I give the original French only of quotations from manuscripts. Heading of Lesson no. 2: "Troisième leçon sanscrite à Monsieur e [*sic*] Madame la Marquise. H. S."

11. "Première leçon de la langue Sanscrite/à Mr. le Marq. De St. Yves D'Alveydre/ Paris ce 8 Juin 1885/Manavirt 25; Mithûna 55,645/de guru Pandit H. S. Bagwandass/de la grande école Agarthienne."

12. See especially Louis Jacolliot, *Le Fils de Dieu* (Paris: Lacroix, 1873), 263–66, quoted in Jean Saunier, *Saint-Yves d'Alveydre, une Synarchie sans énigme* (Paris: Dervy, 1981), 350–53.

13. "Ici selon votre ardent désir, mais cependant vous n'est [*sic*] pas encore assez preparer [*sic*] pour la Vattan (pianô et sanô)." Note that Hardjji misspells French, and quotes an Italian proverb. The Vattanian inscription in this book (see page 40) spells "Marquis de Saint-Yves d'Alveydre" with its lowest symbols, and "Dev Bramha" (To Lord Brahma?) with the top group. I cannot decipher the seven intermediate groups; they may represent the seven sacred hieroglyphs on the Brâhatmah's tiara (see page 91).

14. "Modèle des éléments vattaniques pour le seul rite Agarthien, à l'usage des Initiés."

15. Papus, *Traité élémentaire des sciences occultes* (Paris, 1898), quoted in Saunier, *Saint-Yves d'Alveydre*, 329.

16. Sorbonne Ms. 1824. The Sanskrit notes are in the first two notebooks bound under this call number.

17. "Le gourou notre le nom Hajji Shariph B.V.D. [this name in Sanskrit] de Bombay de l'agarttha cardinale dans l'Inde." ". . . comment a-t-il pu étant sorti d'agarttha." Sorbonne, Ms. 1824, folios 47', 48.

18. "Maître de l'Univers et Protecteur de la terre sainte Agarttha [this word in Vattanian], au nom de l'[Vattanian symbols] moi, qui est le tien et mes pensées sont à toi et en toi. Accordez moi le [symbols] de ta sublime bonté à titre d'un yogi Dwya en âme et corps—de quel voeu je ne me departerais jamais. Om [etc.]."

19. Actually an alphabet called "Adamic script" found in Paul Christian's *Histoire de la Magie* (Paris, 1870).

20. Reproduced in Saint-Yves d'Alveydre's posthumously published work *L'Archéomètre* (Paris: Dorbon, 1911; reprinted Paris: Gutenberg, 1979), 153–54; English translation by Ariel Godwin forthcoming as *The Archeometer: Key to All the Religions and Sciences of Antiquity. Synthetic Reformation of All Contemporary Arts* (n.p.: Sacred Science Institute, 2008).

21. Reprinted in ibid.

22. There are a few more pages of the same kind of material, then the notebook resumes with an entirely new series of notes, dated ten years later (see below).

23. See Saunier, *Saint-Yves d'Alveydre*, 147–54.

24. "Se méfier dans 18 mois ou 2 ans d'un assassinat de ma femme par un russe blond en automne. Rester à pris cet automne près de Marie. A [Venus sign] 17 juin 1887. Somnambule de degio." Sorbonne Ms. 1823, f. 152'. I cannot explain the Vattanian symbols that transliterate as "degio."

25. Saint-Yves d'Alveydre, *Le poème de la Reine/ The Poem of the Queen* (Paris: Lahure, 1889). The poem is in 22 stanzas, each marked by a letter of the Hebrew alphabet. The English translation is by the Earl of Lytton, son of the novelist Bulwer Lytton.

26. Saint-Yves d'Alveydre, *Clefs de l'Orient* (Paris: Didier, 1877; reprinted Nice: Belisane, 1980).

27. "Il a causé avec Papus et Guaïta, dit-il, mais ne leur a pas dit ce qu'ils voulaient savoir: le moyen de se dégager et réengager en corps astral. C'est dangereux, je ne veux pas, m'a-t-il dit, vous mettre en main un revolver chargé dont vous ne sauriez pas vous servir. / Un magnétiseur court, dit-il, moins de dangers que

d'autres à se dédoubler, car il est plus entrainé. / Quand on sort de son corps en Astral, un autre mauvais esprit peut vous remplacer." Sorbonne, Ms. Carton 42, fragment G, [7–8]. Erny was the author of *Le Psychisme experimentale* (Paris: Flammarion, 1895). His handwritten notes on conversations with Saint-Yves, dated August, 1896, are divided between the Sorbonne and the Bibliothèque Municipale de Lyon, Ms. 5493.

28. See the introduction by Jean Saunier to *Mission de l'Inde* (Nice: Bélisane, 1981).

29. Ibid., vii.

30. See the facsimile of Hardjji's letter on pages 162–63.

31. See Saunier, *Saint-Yves d'Alveydre,* 284–86; Léon Cellier, *Fabre d'Olivet: Contribution à l'étude des aspects réligieuses du romantisme* (Paris: Nizet, 1953), 385–88.

32. See Saunier, *Saint-Yves d'Alveydre,* 132–37.

33. They include *Dans la Boue* [In the Mud], *Femme et Prêtre* [Woman and Priest], *Adultère et Divorce* [Adultery and Divorce], and *Haine charnelle* [Carnal Hatred].

34. See Saunier, *Saint-Yves d'Alveydre,* chapter IV; also Jean Saunier, *La Synarchie, ou le vieux rêve d'une nouvelle société* (Paris: Grasset, 1971).

35. Quoted in Saunier, *Saint-Yves d'Alveydre,* 325–27. See pages 165–68.

36. See Jean-Pierre Laurant, *Le Sens caché dans l'oeuvre de René Guénon* (Paris: L'Age d'Homme, 1975), 46–49. The report of the sessions was immediately published in *Hiram,* March, 1909. For further details see Robert Amadou, "L'Erreur spirite de René Guénon," *Sphinx* (Beaugency), no. 3/4 (Autumn 1978): 21 unpaginated pages; no. 5 (Spring 1979): 45–60; no. 7/8 (Autumn/Winter 1979): 83.

37. For an outsider's view of this school, see Mark Sedgwick, *Against the Modern World: Traditionalism and the Secret Intellectual History of the Twentieth Century* (New York: Oxford University Press, 2004).

38. Ferdinand Ossendowski, *Beasts, Men and Gods* (New York: Dutton, 1922). The book was written in English, with assistance from Lewis Stanton Palen.

39. Ibid., 413.

40. "J'aimerais mieux cela!" Quoted in Paul Chacornac, *La Vie simple de René Guénon* (Paris: Editions Traditionnelles, 1958), 77n. However, in November, 1924, when pressed to appear before a group that included Georges Duhamel, Louis Aragon, Pierre Benoit, and the Tibetologist Jacques Bacot, Ossendowski confessed that his book was not "scientific" but "exclusively a literary work,"

and stated the same in a letter to the Royal Geographical Society. See the anonymous review, "The Ossendowski Controversy," *The Geographical Journal* 65, no. 3 (1925): 251–54, which reproduces Ossendowski's statements in French and English.

41. René Guénon, "Le Roi du Monde," *Les Cahiers du Mois,* 9/10: *Les Appels de l'Orient* (Paris: Emile Paul Frères, 1925): 210. This statement was modified in Guénon's *Le Roi du Monde* (Paris: Bosse, 1927); see next note.

42. René Guénon, *The Lord of the World,* trans. Anthony Cheke (Ellingstring: Coombe Springs Press, 1983), 2–3.

43. Ibid., 66.

44. Laurant, *René Guénon,* 136.

45. *Beasts, Men and Gods,* 304.

46. "Les sources d'Ossendowsky," see note 7, above.

47. E.g., Jean Robin, *René Guénon, témoin de la tradition* (Paris: Laffont, 1978), 316–17.

48. Quoted in Saunier, *Saint-Yves d'Alveydre,* 366–67.

49. See Jean Robin, *René Guénon,* 58; Pierre Geyraud, *Les Sociétés secrètes de Paris* (Paris: Emile Paul Frères, 1938), 57; Zam Bhotiva (pseudonym of Cesare Accomani), *Asia mysteriosa* (Paris: Dorbon Ainé, 1929).

50. *Asia Mysteriosa,* 86.

51. "Those things that are above are like unto those things that are below; and those things that are below are like unto those things that are above."

52. Jean Marquès-Rivière, in *Asia Mysteriosa,* 26.

53. Jean Marquès-Rivière, *A l'ombre des monastères tibétains* (Paris & Neuchâtel: Victor Attinger, 7th ed., 1930), 198. Jean-Pierre Laurant, in his summary of *Le Roi du Monde,* mentions a curious parallel in the "Agartus oppidum" near the Nile, mentioned by the third-century writer Lucius Ampelius (Laurant, *René Guénon,* 129).

54. The relationship of Agarttha to Shambhala, the spiritual city of Tibetan Buddhism, is a recurrent topos of popular occult writers. Some of them state that the word "Agarttha" appears in *The Way to Shambhala,* written in 1774 by the Third Panchen Lama. However, I have not found it in the scholarly edition, with German translation, by Albert Grünwedel, *Der Weg nach Śambala* (Munich, 1915). Further on the Polaires and other examples of polar mythology, as well as myths of the inner or hollow earth and its reputed inhabitants, see my *Arktos* (see note 1, above) and the many references given there.

55. An exception is Walter Kafton-Minkel, *Subterranean Worlds: 100,000 years of dragons, dwarfs, the dead, lost races & UFOs from inside the earth* (Port Townsend, WA: Loompanics Unlimited, 1989), a cheerful and accurate survey of the myth from a Fortean viewpoint.

56. Louis Jacolliot, *Les Fils de Dieu* (Paris: Lacroix, 1873), 263–65, 272, 310–12.

57. Jean Reyor, "L'Archéomètre de Saint-Yves d'Alveydre," *La Voile d'Isis* 40 (July 1935): 287.

58. Preface by "XXX," identifiable because it reuses verbatim parts of Reyor's article cited above.

59. "Enseignement secret des Brahmes à moi communiqué par le Rishi," etc.

60. Sorbonne, Ms. 1823, 41.

61. *Mission des Juifs,* vol. 1, 84–96.

62. The letter is not included in the volume *The Mahatma Letters* (see note 64, below), but is in A. P. Sinnett, *The Occult World*, 7th ed. (Boston: Houghton, Mifflin, 1897), 125–39.

63. For a speculative but very stimulating account, see K. Paul Johnson, *The Masters Revealed. Madame Blavatsky and the Myth of the Great White Lodge* (Albany: State University of New York Press, 1994).

64. So writes Mahatma Morya in Letter No. 44, in *The Mahatma Letters to A. P. Sinnett from the Mahatmas M. and K. H.,* 3rd ed., edited by Christmas Humphreys and Elsie Benjamin (Adyar: Theosophical Publishing House, 1979), 259.

65. *L'Archéomètre,* 108.

66. Jean Reyor, article cited above, note 34. See also the important anonymous reply, "À propos de Saint-Yves d'Alveydre," *La Voile d'Isis* 41 (March 1936): 108–13.

67. On Vattanian, see Mike Jay and Joscelyn Godwin, "Licked by the Mother Tongue," *Fortean Times* 97 (April 1997).

THE
KINGDOM
OF
AGARTTHA

—⚬—

PREFACE

I have long hesitated before writing these pages, torn between emotions of anxiety, humility, and the complete annihilation of myself.

An invincible resolve enabled me to take a stand, certain of the good I would be doing, not only for the noble minds who have supported my earlier works, but for the peoples of the two parts of the world I am addressing in this book.*

But first and foremost I wish to express my profound gratitude to the elite intellects and souls who have had the courage to testify publicly in writing of their approval of the physical law of History and human societies: Synarchy, in other words the opposite of Anarchy.

In this constitutional process, the former President of the Bar of Paris, Ernest Desmarest, and Hippolyte Destrem, author of *Perte ou salut de la France* [Ruin or Salvation of France], have witnessed the methodical reorganization of international relations (*Minutes of the Congress of Brussels, Petit Républicain, la Presse* [Little Republican, the Press]).

His Lordship Count Charles de Montblanc has recognized therein the scientific law of history and that of the Self-Government† of societies (*Le Figaro*).

His Lordship Baron Theodore de Cambourg took particular note

---

*[Asia and Europe, per the book's title in French: Mission de l'Inde en Europe; Mission de l'Europe en Asie. —*Trans.*]

†[English in original. —*Trans.*]

therein of national representation through their specialties as well as of what I call the third Chamber. He has made himself the apostle for the creation of a Chamber for the National Economy, whose purpose is to balance the politics inspired by the passions of each party by adjusting the weight of all their competing interests (*Gazette de France*).

In the Synarchic process, the Canon Roca, former laureate of the school of advanced studies of the Carmelites, has noted the possibility of an organic reconciliation between faith and science; between the ecclesiastical teaching bodies and the universities; and between the various forms of worship and secular society (*La Crise fatale et le salut d'Europe* [The Fatal Crisis and Salvation of Europe]; *La fin de l'ancien monde* [The end of the Old World]).

The Reverend Father Curci has seen in it a desirable intellectual and social government; he has no fear of advocating the attempt to establish such an entity (*Il Socialismo cristiano* [Christian Socialism]).

Pastor de la Fresnaye has rediscovered in it the Judeo-Christian termination of history as well as the positive law of solidarity (*Courrier de la Gironde**).

Isaac Levy, Grand Rabbi of Vesoul, took particular note of the reconciliation of reason with faith, the concern of a government capable of guaranteeing the happiness of humanity, and the mutual peace between religions and teachings (*Famille de Jacob* [Jacob's Family]).

Louis Pauliat found confirmation in it of his belief in the return to a universal Synarchy (*Nouvelle Revue* [New Review]).

Charles Limousin had no fear of revealing the profound impression that the reading of the *Missions*† made on his mind (*Revue du mouvement social* [Review of Social Movement]).

René Caillé, an engineer, and Barlet, a licensed attorney, discovered in these books everything that tends to bring back to life the spirit

---

*[Newspaper for Gironde, a region of southwest France. —*Ed.*]

†[Saint-Yves' other *Missions* (of the Sovereigns, of the Workers, of the Jews) have not yet been translated into English. The French versions have all seen various reprintings since their original publication; all are somewhat rare, but not impossible to find. —*Ed.*]

of the ancient temple universities in which science and faith were one (*Anti-matérialiste* [Anti-Materialist]).

Monsieur de Sant-Albano sees in Synarchy the realization of the promises of Moses and the Christ, in which those of the 1789 revolution reemerge* (*Le High-Life*).

His Highness the Prince of Z. considers European Synarchy to be the necessary conclusion of the intergovernmental constitution inaugurated in 1648 by the Congress of Westphalia (*Revue Internationale de Florence* [International Review of Florence]).

Fabre des Essarts, taking a purely French and Republican perspective, has inaugurated a series of popular publications entitled *Bibliothèque synarchique* [Synarchic Library]. In his first pamphlet, *La Force, le Droit et les trois Chambres synarchiques* [The Force, the Law, and the Three Synarchic Chambers], he took pains to emphasize the necessity of arming universal suffrage with a triple representation through the channel of specialties and skills.

I deeply regret being unable to cite all the other public testimonies that my *Missions* have elicited.

However, I cannot pass over in silence those given by the *Revue moderne* and the *Moniteur universal,* the latter of which was the work of an eminent university professor whom I wish not to name because of his official position.

Lastly, His Lordship the Baron Theodore de Combourg, Destrem, Garreau (general commissioner of marine affairs), and Marty (one of the presidents of the labor union), as well as Count Charles de Montblanc, have all given extensive study to the possibility of creating one of the three Synarchic Chambers, the Chamber in charge of the national economy (*Projet d'une Union économique française* [Plan for a French Economic Union]).

Thanks to these generous endorsements, I will be in more fortunate straits than Kepler, and will not die saying: "One reader in one hundred years!"

---

*[French revolution. —*Trans.*]

Not only have I been read by an intellectual elite who are conscious of the good I wish to do, but I have had the rare good fortune to see my thought come to life in these people and be transmitted into action under the impetus of their enlightened love for our country and humanity.

May I be permitted to express to them all my grateful affection.

A seed of social salvation sprouting in such good soil can henceforth not perish.

In addition to these public testimonies, I also wish to thank all those who in their letters or in person have given me such powerful encouragement, and if I refrain from naming the dearest and most flattering of these, it is out of a feeling of reserve, which I know they will appreciate.

I offer my book to all as proof to them of the perseverance of my efforts, which is the best means I have of thanking them for their indescribable support.

The names I have cited earlier offer the very noteworthy feature of belonging to members of all our religious denominations, our secular teaching establishment, our civil classes, and our political parties.

Synarchy is therefore a terrain for reconciliation as well as social salvation in one and all nations.

This is also the reason why my work has had the honor of receiving such violent attacks.

For example, from the Carpeaux group,* my *Mission of the Jews* has received its share of inkpots slung at it.

Just as I have listed my work's endorsements, so here I shall list its criticisms.

1. The Celtic origin of the Aryas and the Cycle of Ram are a fiction plagiarized from Fabre d'Olivet, whom I did not even cite.
2. There was no real science in the temples of antiquity.
3. To speak of religion and theocracy is to speak of ignorance and tyranny.

---

*[Sculpture by Jean-Baptiste Carpeaux (1827–1875). —*Trans.*]

4. The esotericism of the sacred texts of all peoples is a product of the imagination of the medieval Kabbalists and hides no true science.

That is the indictment; here is my defense.

So many strong statements; so many errors.

The Cycle of Ram and its Western origin is a historical reality for which all India, in combination with Central Asia, is still witness and guarantor.

As for Fabre d'Olivet, he was no more a fiction-writer than I.

I have verified his sources and cited them twice in *Mission of the Jews,* once specifically in connection with the Celtic Cycle of Ram, which d'Olivet personally discovered among the Indologists of the School of Calcutta.

I add, so as to send to the bottom of the seas this politicking torpedo of plagiarism, that a universal history can only be real on condition of being a universal plagiarism of the ideas and events of the whole of humanity, something over which no person can claim to hold a monopoly.

With respect to the modern world, I only claim absolute paternity in my work for the Synarchic Law that is both theocratic and democratic, as I have defined and demonstrated, even to excess.

With respect to Antiquity, this law can be found there, not only in all the sacred Dorian texts but also in the social constitution as well as the organization of the general government of the Ramid Cycle.

In the presence of a discovery, an insight as capital for historical science as it is for the governmental notions that naturally follow from it, I have been compelled in my work to place the Synarchic Law outside of all sects, doctrines, and specific systems.

It has also been my duty not to submit it, nor my work that demonstrates it, to any authority other than itself, the sacred texts, and the positive history of all peoples.

I would have dealt a crippling blow to the scientific and universal value of this law by pledging fealty to any doctrinaire modern writer, Fabre d'Olivet or any other, whatever admiration I may profess for him, however useful his works may have been for me among the multitude of systems that I have consulted and gone into more deeply.

If I had acted otherwise, the same detractors of my works would not have failed to hurl at my head the biographies and bibliographies in which Fabre d'Olivet's contemporaries slew him under a torrent of scorn and ridicule.

Were they right? No, of course not.

I will one day revisit this matter, but, for the moment, I am obliged to note that the personal and metaphysical system of Fabre d'Olivet is anti-Christian and antidemocratic, which is to say the opposite of my works, of Synarchy, and of my complete detachment from any individual system.

Second allegation: *There was no real science in the temples of antiquity.*

The present book will crown, I hope, the countless proofs that I have already furnished to combat this error.

Tertio: *To speak of religion and theocracy is to speak of ignorance and tyranny.*

If one means by religion a political clericalism and not a social synthesis, if one means by theocracy mutual intolerance of sects and not the divine law of this synthesis, then this statement would be correct.

But it is exactly the opposite of the Synarchic constitution of the Cycle of Ram, as it is of the movement of the Abramites, Moses, and Our Lord Jesus Christ.

Quarto: *The esotericism of the sacred texts of all peoples is a product of the imagination of the medieval Kabbalists and hides no true science.*

I have already shown in my book *Mission of the Jews* what one should think of this error, one, which the present book seeks to dissipate entirely.

Now, if someone should ask me why, having cited the names of my supporters, I do not list those of my detractors, I would answer that my *Missions* are works of universal, social peace and that they bind me personally to this peace.

I know my friends, I do not acknowledge or remember my enemies.

The book I publish today will place upon my previous *Missions* the seal of an undeniable authority. However, by the same token, it is going to project a brilliant light and, momentarily, a profound disturbance in the vast centers of hermetically sealed initiation where the ancient Tradition has been preserved intact over the cycles of the centuries by millions of initiates, who are certainly not expecting me to divulge the information that appears in this book.

Also, being deeply aware of Asian reserve and thereby feeling the full scope of my action, I have no hesitation in saying that this act forms in itself a coup d'État just as significant as all those ever carried out by political men, ever since the fate of humanity was delivered into their hands.

The majority of European readers will greet this declaration with a skeptical half-smile, but this will certainly not be the reaction of the millions of Asiatic initiates who will read, translate, or comment on this book.

They will anxiously wonder what effect the exactitude of this book's revelations will produce in the upper spheres of the religious denominations, the universities, Freemasonry, and certain European courts, two in particular.

They will finally endeavor to find how I managed to pull back the veil that covers the most secret of their mysteries, something that all the combined efforts of missionaries and diplomats have been unable to achieve.

In fact, this veil is formed by immense mountains, fortresses, jungles, cities, temples, crypts, and underground cities of formidable size.

And the secret this veil covers is guarded by millions of men of science and conscience linked together in the heart of the Godhead by the same oaths sworn in the times of Moses, Jethro, Orpheus, Zoroaster, and Fo-Hi.

So, despite the skepticism this book might encounter in Europe, it is impossible to describe the ideopsychic commotion that it will create, visibly or not, throughout the whole of Asia.

From the peak of Ram to Peking, from the Indian Ocean to the Himalayas, from Afghanistan to the plateaus of Upper Tartary,* from Bukharia to Tbilisi, my frail breath growing with the distance will transform into a spiritual tempest, and the eddies of souls will again surge back from Jerusalem to Cairo and to Mecca, from the Geonim to the Imams and from the Chief of the Druzes in Lebanon to the Chief Ganzibra of the Subba of Baghdad, who are descendents of the former Essene disciples of Saint John the Baptist.

To this vast ocean of souls I will make my pious response: "God wishes it to be so, for the time is at hand!"

With respect to myself, I would be the last of the infidels if, keeping for my own use such secrets, I gave thought only to my own risk when universal salvation is at stake.

What have I to fear from men? Nothing.

From God? One thing only: to fail at the task his mercy has deigned to impose upon me.

I fear nothing from men, because I do not define death as a subject for fear.

Whatever happiness God may grant him in this world, every initiate knows that death is an inexpressible bliss of the soul, the greatest voluptuous pleasure it is capable of experiencing.

Courage is needed only to resist it.

I fear nothing from men because my *Missions* have the divine love of humanity as their guiding principle, universal Synarchy as their objective, and they cause risk only to my person.

I fear nothing from men, for I neither expect nor desire anything for myself.

Following what I have just said, it would be puerile to add that I am

---

*[Name once given by Europeans to the vast Asian region between the Ural Mountains and the Pacific Ocean, including but not limited to parts of Siberia, Mongolia, Manchuria, and Turkestan. —*Trans.*]

resigned at most, and insensitive at the least, and that the half-scholars, atheists, and sectarian enemies of all worship and of all faith, who hope to reduce the scope of my actions through mockery or insult, can only arouse my pity.

I have said that I fear nothing from men.

There is one, however, whom I might dread.

This man would be me, if I had anything for which to reproach my conscience or if I were in violation of the oath of a human initiation by publishing this crowning work of my *Missions*.

This is not the case at all. God alone, through the heavens as in the depths of the history of humanity, is the Living Presence from whom I have received the Synarchic Law in my religious comprehension of the social promise of Our Lord Jesus Christ, Moses, the Abramites, as well as that later Communion of the Ramids that Saint Paul calls the Society of the Protogonos, and which I have called elsewhere by its antique name the *Paradesa*.

When I said in *Mission of the Sovereigns* and *Mission of the Jews* that everything I was reserving for the reconstruction of the edifice of the Sciences in a Chamber of Teaching, following the establishment of Synarchy, was being kept in safe hands in several different countries, I had serious reasons for being so explicit.

Today, after much deliberation, I corroborate this promise, while adding that the Ramid Paradesa, its university temple, its traditions, and the quadruple hierarchy of its teaching still exist, unchanged, at the current time.

It is to its Sovereign Pontiff that I permit myself to respectfully dedicate this book.

—–—

To the Sovereign Pontiff who wears the
seven-crowned tiara of the current Brâhatmah
of the ancient metropolitan Paradesa of
the Cycle of the Lamb and Aries.

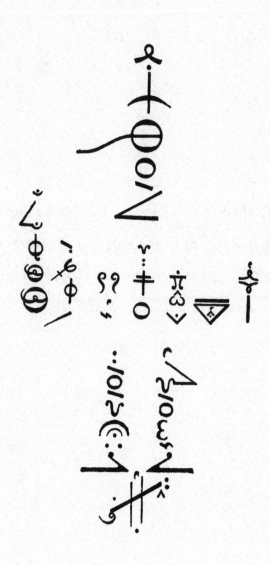

Ah! I know; when his eyes fall on these pages, he will ask God and his Angels if the impossible can have been achieved.

"How is it," he will ask himself, "that a human eye has taken me by surprise in the most secret of my sealed sanctuaries, in the most formidable of my sciences, my arts, and my Pontifical mysteries?

"Will I not then be safer, when beneath the eyes of the Eternal Living Presence and face to face with his cosmic powers, I breathe past death inside the flaming soul of the world where I shall speak from star to star with the Pontiffs who preceded me?"

Perhaps then the word profanation will rise to his pious lips, but little by little, as he reads me, he will find reassurance.

Indeed, be reassured, great and holy soul who is completely resplendent with the Wisdom and Knowledge of the ancient initiations.

It is with deeply emotional respect that I cast my eyes upon you from the depths of this West that was the cradle of Ram.

And I see you at this very moment, in your ascetic leanness, a true statue of dark bronze with crossed arms over the tomb of your predecessor that lies in the sacred crypt, which is impenetrable even to the initiates of high degree.

Be reassured, Eldest of the days of this plane, it is a religious soul that visits you, worshipping in you the spirit of all the ancient times and the formidable Sapience to which you have been guided by degrees over a fearsome ascent of ordeals and teachings that are both natural and human, and cosmogonic and divine.

It was in fact from your living temple that the Magi Kings came to worship in his cradle the sorrowful Christ, the divine incarnation of the eternally glorious Christ.

And it is as a Catholic Synarchist that I place myself beneath the invocation of these same Magi, in order to make my way to you across this vast stretch, to bring to you, full of faith, love, and hope, the promise of this Christ, with what I firmly believe to be the law of his social fulfillment for all humanity.

CHAPTER ONE

Within the most ancient university of Earth resides the authority who stands as guarantor of the oldest Tradition of Antiquity, and of all concerning what I have said elsewhere about the intellectual and social formation of the Cycle of the Lamb and Aries.

At the time I write these lines, all the teaching bodies of the world mark their ages in the following manner:

Those of Mohammed: 1264
Those of Jesus Christ: 1886
Those of Moses: 5647
Finally those of Manu: 55647

I respectfully accept all of these dates, to which I might have added the eras of Çakya Muni,* Zoroaster, Fo-Hi, Christna, and finally the Ramid Cycle, if they did not fall within the entire period of Manu.

Far from horrifying my Christian faith, the immensity of the Manavic date instead gives it reassurance, by extending so far into the past the grandeur of the human mind, which is inseparable from the majesty of the divine traditions.

---

*["Çakya Muni" refers to the person we commonly know as the Buddha, also known as Sakyamuni, Siddhartha Gautama, Gautama Buddha, etc. —*Ed.*]

Here, I would like to pause a moment to discuss my previous book: *Mission of the Jews.*

Despite the discoveries made by archaeologists since the end of the last century,* despite the introduction into Europe since that time of fairly numerous literary fragments of what the Brahmas believe they can safely make public without betraying their oaths, the Cycle of Ram, although it merely goes back nine thousand years, still finds skeptics in Europe.

However, even in Paris itself, the catalogs of Sanskrit manuscripts from the Bibliothèque Orientale, not to mention the earlier works of Herbelot, have given indication, since the beginning of this century, of countless works on Ram and on the heroes after him, who deserve incorporation into his legend. Such works include the *Veyasa-Ramayana, Vasista-Ramayana, Adhyatma-Ramayana, Hanumad-Ramayana, Sata-Kanta-Ramayana, Sahasra-Kanta-Ramayana, Djimoun-Ramayana, Valmike-Ramayana,* and so on.

This last work, the most noteworthy of them all, was written by Valmiki toward the end of the Trata Yuga under the reign of the Ramas.

This magnificent poem itself is merely an abridgment of the *Veyasa-Ramayana,* an account of Rama's actions in ten trillion verses, a work that has long been reserved in India for the esoteric study of history.

The authors I cited in *Mission of the Jews,* who considered the traditions of the Brahmanic East to be an integral part of universal history, were thus perfectly justified—as am I who follow in their footsteps—in restoring to the Cycle of Ram the importance it is still granted by a vast portion of the human race.

In my last volume, whose true title should actually have been *The Positive History of Synarchy and Anarchy in the General Governing of the World,* I did not go any farther back than ninety centuries.

However, this was not because documents were lacking that would enable one to go beyond that era into the very depths of time.

---

*[Saint-Yves, writing in 1886, was naturally referring to the end of the eighteenth century here. —*Ed.*]

The annals of humanity, for the five hundred and fifty-six centuries since their transition upon this earth from a natural state to a social state, are piously guarded in inaccessible places, about which I will speak more later.

But I must limit myself to providing European readers with a scientific demonstration of Synarchy, by reminding them of their own Synarchic annals.

They date, in fact, to the time when their race, having gained dominance over the others, rose up in the person of the greatest of their Celtic heroes to take the seven-crowned tiara of the sanctuaries of Manu, obtaining the imperial hand of Justice of the ancient Kingdom of God.

The initiates of Paradesa certainly did not snicker at the Cycle of Ram, its dates, and its Synarchy realizing anew this divine rule that has endured three thousand years; nor did they scoff at its colossal civilization, its four scientific hierarchies ranging from the secret depths of physical Nature to the ineffable essence of the Cosmogonic Powers; nor, finally, at its arts and all the dazzling Mysteries celebrated in its metropolises that are both religious centers and universities.

These initiates have not cast doubt on all I have said about the revolution of the third Orders at the call of Irshu, and about the Synarchic emperor Ougra, nor scoffed at the consecutive assaults suffered by the Ramid Synarchy of the Lamb and the Zodiacal Ram at the hands of the growing anarchy of the Turanians, Yonijas, Hiksos, and Phoenicians, displaying the bloody standard of the Bull as the rallying symbol of their naturalism.

Nor have these initiates charged with inexactitude the entire History of the General Government of the World, starting from the time when, under the impetus of a multitudinous force, the regime of the arbitrary condemned by Moses under the name of Nimrod, the Way of the Tiger, was enthroned there.

Nor have these initiates denied the consistently illuminating and tirelessly liberating role played by the Sanctuaries, which seek to remedy everywhere the apotheosis of the triumphant power and prepare all places for the return of the condition of the ancient universal Covenant.

Finally, they have certainly not found it in themselves to contradict what I have said about the scientific Hermeticism of the Dorian languages, which are the exact mirror of the eternal Logos,* nor what I have said of the splendid esotericism that is contained in the true sacred texts not only of the Vedas, not only in the books of the first Zoroaster and of Hermes, but also in the hieratic Hebrew of the Fifty Chapters of Moses† and the divine Testament of Our Lord Jesus Christ.

All of these things, in fact, and many others besides, are still taught in the absolute purity of an uninterrupted tradition in the depths of the Sanctuaries of the Lamb; and these latter are none but the crypt that has been sealed until my efforts, containing the Mysteries of the revolving movement of the Abramites, of Moses, and finally of the universal promise made to humanity by the divine teacher of all the Christians.

And if one were to ask me why the Pontiffs of Paradesa, showing no pity for the gigantic efforts made by a large portion of our race, have hidden their religious university from the eyes of humanity, I would answer:

They had good reason to do so, because their formidable sciences, much as our own have done, would have provided a weapon to be used against humanity by Evil, the Antigod, the Antichrist, and the general government of Anarchy.

Yes, they were right to do so, inasmuch as the conditions of universal Synarchy have not yet been sufficiently restored over the surface of the entire globe, even with the initiative of the Abramites, Moses, and Jesus.

These sacred names, which I will speak and repeat often, do not

---

*[The "Word" mentioned at the beginning of *Genesis*; *Verbe* in French. —*Ed.*]
†[i.e., *Genesis*. —*Ed.*]

involve in my thought, no more than they do in that of the dwellers of Paradesa, any of the political or sectarian notions that ignorance has lent to them.

On the contrary, they signify the universal return of humanity to the divine Law that presided over its organization.

Far from casting anathema on any religion, Paradesa blesses all of them and reserves to all of them the justification of all their sacred texts, all their sacraments, and all their Mysteries.

I need only show as evidence our own holy gospel, which, in its Hebrew text, relates the mystical name of the temple of Paradesa and the significant words of Our Lord Jesus Christ: "Ask and you shall receive, knock and the door shall be opened, seek and you shall find."

Our Savior and, before him, the esoteric teaching colleges known under the names of the Prophets, Moses, Jethro, and the various patriarchs, never spoke words in vain. Everyone knows as well as I inside what living Tabernacle Providence keeps safe the ancient seeds of future civilizations.

In the time preceding ours, Paradesa was compelled not to impose but to suffer the law of the Mysteries dictated by God himself to this ancient metropolis of the religious universities, starting at the time when the governmental Anarchy of Nimrod destroyed the relationship then existing between all human societies.

This same law of the Mysteries will only be gradually abrogated, and that only when the promises of Moses and Jesus Christ are made good by the Judeo-Christians, when the Anarchy of the general government of humanity gives way to Synarchy, and when the fatal yoke of the Antichrist and the Antigod are replaced by Liberty, Equality, and Fraternity of nations in the Kingdom of God through the action of Christ.

As for me, after having armed the Judeo-Christians with all the social meanings behind their traditions, it is Paradesa itself that I will take as guarantor of the truth of my earlier testimonies and of its own existence.

And if, finding me too well informed of the greatest secrets of their arts, sciences, and mysteries, these initiated scholars are driven to seek my name in their registries and my statue in their underground cities, they will find naught but my spirit that appeared there close to ten years ago, so clearly that my portrait could have been drawn from it.

Nevertheless, as a spontaneous initiate, I have never at any time in my life given any teaching body, nor any individual, any manner of oath pledging not to reveal whatever I might learn or grasp in order to do good to my fellow humans.

This is another reason for me to remain silent concerning all that might cause true harm to the metropolitan temple of Paradesa, *at the closed zero of the twenty-two Mysteries.*

If the independent rajahs in Asia who still form part of the Council of the Gods, and the Pundits and Gurus, the Bhagwans and Archis, who, with the Brâhatmah and his two assessors, make up the Manavic Council of God, find a kind of precision that initially offends them in what I have just written and what will follow, then I assume complete and total responsibility for it.

All that I am about to say is only the development of my earlier work, and nobody but me, among those yet living, should be accused of indiscretion.

I do not owe my Synarchic enlightenment about the past and about the present to any Asiatic initiate currently living, but to several clues vouchsafed me by an august departed individual about whom I have spoken in *Mission of the Jews.*

So there should be no grounds for suspicion of any intentional revelation, no matter how large or small it may be.

As for those currently living initiates whom I have been fortunate enough to know, they unlocked their lips only because I told them in advance the knowledge that they dreaded to offer me.

I have seen them throw themselves to their knees before God, carried away by ecstasy, while asserting amidst their sobs that it was God himself who forced them to speak.

— —

I hasten to add, to the glory of Paradesa, that these meetings have always been an austere and holy joy for me, an inestimable conformation; and that those of its residents whom it has allowed me to know have always increased, through their wisdom and learning, their holiness, and all their virtues, the respect that I profess for the Ancestor of all temples, all universities, and all civilizations.

I affirm and swear by my soul's salvation that not a person in the world was aware of my intention to write this book and that I have taken counsel from God alone.

Finally, without seeking to explain myself more clearly, I hereby inform the residents of Paradesa that my religious audacity, which they will perhaps fault as mad temerity, is yet only, as far as they are concerned, an act of preservation, prudence, and salvation, whose value they will one day appreciate.

With that said, the reader can now follow me into the metropolitan sanctuary of the Cycle of Ram.

THE MYSTIC SANCTUARY

The current mystical name of this Temple was given to it following the schism of Irshu almost fifty-one centuries ago.

This name, Agarttha, आगरर्थ, means inaccessible to violence and inaccessible to Anarchy.

This hierogram alone gives the key to the response made by the Trinitarian Synarchy of the Lamb and Aries to the triumph of the general government of brute force, whether it go by the name of military conquest, political tyranny, sectarian intolerance, or colonial rapacity.

Where is Agarttha? What is the specific region in which it lies? Along what road, through what civilizations, must one walk in order to reach it?

It is not suitable for me to answer these questions, which diplomats and military men alike will not fail to ask, at any greater length than I am about to do in this book, before a Synarchic understanding has been reached or at least a treaty signed toward that end.

But since I know that certain powers, in their competition with each other across the whole of Asia, will undoubtedly come close to this sacred territory, and since I know that in some future conflict their armies will inevitably seek to approach it and even to enter it, I have no fear of continuing the divulgation I have begun—out of humanity both for these European peoples and for Agarttha itself.

On the surface and in the bowels of the earth, the true extent of Agarttha defies the embrace and the constraint of profanation and violence.

In Asia alone there are a half a billion people who are more or less aware of its existence and its greatness—not to mention America, whose subterranean regions belonged to Agarttha in very remote antiquity.

But nowhere will there be found among them a traitor who would provide the precise location where its Council of God and its Council of Gods, its pontifical head and its judicial heart, are located.

If this were to somehow happen nonetheless, and if Agarttha were invaded despite its numerous and terrible defenders, every conquering army, even if it consisted of a million men, would see a repetition of the thundering response of the Temple of Delphi to the countless hordes sent by the Persian satraps.

By calling to their aid the cosmic powers of Earth and Heaven, the Templars and the confederates of Agarttha, even in defeat, could blow up a part of the planet if necessary, destroying these profaners and their country of origin in a cataclysm.

It is for these reasons that the central portion of this sacred earth has never been profaned, despite the ebb and flow, the mutual shock and collapse of military empires from Babylon to the Turanian Kingdom of Upper Tartary, from Susa to Pella, from Alexandria to Rome.

— —

Before Ram's expedition and the predominance of the white race in Asia, the center of the Manavic metropolis was Ayodhya, the Solar City.

With a sure knowledge of Europe's true frontier in Asia, our Celtic ancestor established the Sacred College in the most splendid sites the earth has to offer, and sat at its head as the culmination of his initiatory path.

The earlier libraries remained unchanged, thanks to his very knowledge, despite all the intellectual and social forms created by his luminous initiative.

More than three thousand years after the time of Ram, beginning with the schism of Irshu, the university center of the Synarchy of the Lamb and Aries underwent its first relocation, about which it is not my place to divulge any further detail.

Finally, close to fourteen centuries after Irshu, and a short time after Çakya Muni, the decision for another change of location was made.

Let it be sufficient for my readers to know that in certain regions of the Himalayas, among the twenty-two temples representing the twenty-two Mysteries of Hermes and the twenty-two letters of certain sacred alphabets, the Agarttha forms the mystical zero, which is to be found nowhere.

The Zero, which is to say All or Nothing, all because of the harmonic unity and nothing without it, and all because of Synarchy and nothing because of Anarchy.

The sacred territory of Agarttha is independent, organized in accordance with Synarchic principles, and consists of a population that has grown to approach twenty million souls.

The constitution of the family, with equality of sexes in the home, and the organization of civic communities, cantons, and representational districts from the Provincial level to that of the central government, still retain in all their purity the imprint of the Celtic genius of Ram grafted upon the divine wisdom of the institutions of Manu.

I will not enter into greater detail here, as this topic will be generously examined elsewhere.

In all human societies, the statistics of crime, poverty, and prostitution give proof of their physical vices.

None of our frightful judicial or penitentiary systems are known in Agarttha: there are no prisons.

The death penalty is not applied there.

The duties of the police are carried out by the family fathers.

Crimes are referred to the initiates and to the pundits who oversee this duty.

Their peace arbitration, which is always spontaneously requested by the parties themselves, in almost every case prevents any appeal to the various courts of justice, for the reason that voluntary reparation immediately follows any harm or damage.

Need I say that all the shames and social plagues of non-Synarchic societies—mass poverty, prostitution, drunkenness, ferocious individualism among the upper classes, subversive spirit among the lower classes, and negligent behavior of all manner—are unknown in this ancient Synarchy?

The independent rajahs, who are all officers of the various representational districts of the sacred land, are all initiates of high degree.

These kings preside over the Supreme Court of Justice, and their arbitration, established above the cantonal republics, still retains that magisterial nature I examined with such depth in *Mission of the Jews.*

Around this sacred territory and its already considerable population, there extends a Synarchic confederation of peoples, whose total population is greater than forty million souls.

It is with this shield that European conquerors will have to deal initially, trying in vain to win through force what only a loyal alliance can give them.

And if they are successful at breaking this living rampart, they will find themselves face to face, as I have said earlier, with tragic surprises as colossal as that of the Temple of Delphi, and with soldiers who come back to life without cease, linked together like the warriors of Thermopylae, some of whom, like these latter, will regather their forces after death to fight the Profaners again within the very heart of the Invisible Realm.

Castes, a subject of rightful criticism for the Europeans, are unknown in Agarttha.

The child of the least of Hindu pariahs could gain admission into the sacred University, and, depending on his merits, could leave it or remain to go through all the degrees of the hierarchy.

The presentation is made in the following manner.

At the time of a child's birth, he or she is dedicated by his or her mother: this is the Nazarite of all the Temples of the cycle of the Lamb.

At different stages in succession, Providence is interrogated directly in the Temples, and when the age of admission has arrived, the boy or girl, whose godfather in this endeavor is the initiated rajah of the province, enters the Sacred University, with all expenses absolutely covered.

The rest depends only upon his or her personal merit.

I will now describe the central organization of Agarttha, working my way from bottom to top or from the circumference to the center.

Millions of Dwijas, हिजाँ, *twice born,* and Yogis, योगिं, *one with God,* form the great circle, or semicircle rather, that we are about to enter.

They inhabit entire cities. These municipalities are the interior suburbs of Agarttha, symmetrically divided and portioned out in constructions that are mostly underground.

Above them, and heading toward the center, we find five thousand pundits, pandavan, पन्दवाँ, *scholars,* some among whom indeed provide the service of teaching, while others serve as soldiers of the interior police or the police of the five gates.

Their number of five thousand corresponds to the number of Hermetic roots of the Vedic language.

Each root is itself a magic hierogram, connected to a celestial power, with the sanction of an infernal power.

Agarttha in its entirety is a faithful image of the eternal Logos throughout the whole of Creation.

After the pundits, we next find, divided into semicircles of increasingly reduced size, the solar circumscriptions of the three hundred and sixty-five Bagwandas, बघ्न्दाँ, *cardinals*.

The highest circle, closest to the mysterious center, consists of twelve members.

These latter individuals represent the supreme Initiation and correspond, among other things, to the Zone of the Zodiac.

In the celebration of their magic Mysteries, they wear the hieroglyphs of the signs of the Zodiac. They also wear certain hieratic letters, which can be seen in all the ornamentation of their temples and sacred objects.

Each of these Bagwandas or supreme gurus (guru means teacher) bears seven names, hierograms, or mentrams of the seven terrestrial, infernal, or celestial powers.

I will restrict myself to revealing but one of the objects of this power.

The libraries that contain the true body of all the ancient arts and sciences of the last five hundred and fifty-six centuries are inaccessible to any profane sight or any manner of attack.

They are only to be found in the bowels of the earth.

With respect to matters concerning the Cycle of Ram, they occupy some of the underground caverns of the former empire of Aries and its colonies.

The libraries of the earlier Cycles are to be found beneath the seas that swallowed up the ancient Southern continent and in the subterranean constructions of ancient antediluvian America.

What I am about to relate both here and throughout the book will seem like a story straight from *One Thousand and One Nights,* yet nothing could be more real.

The actual university archives of Paradesa occupy thousands of miles. For cycles of many centuries, several high initiates possessing the secrets of only certain religions, and knowing the true purpose of certain works, have been obliged, beginning each year, to spend three years carving on stone tablets all the facts concerning the four hierarchies of sciences forming the total corpus of Knowledge.

Each one of these scholars performs his work in solitude, far from any visible light, beneath the cities, deserts, plains, or mountains.

The reader should picture in his mind a colossal chessboard that extends under the earth's surface to cover almost every region of the Globe.

All the splendors of Humanity's time on earth can be found in each square of this chessboard. In some squares the encyclopedias of the centuries and millennia are located, while in others, lastly, are those of the major and minor Yugas.

On the day when Europe finally replaces the anarchy of its general Government with Trinitarian Synarchy, all of these marvels as well as a good many others will become spontaneously accessible to the representatives of its first amphictyonic Chamber: the Chamber of Teaching.

But until then, woe to the curious and the careless who endeavor to scour the earth!

Only the Sovereign Pontiff of Agarttha with his principal assessors, about whom I will speak in greater detail later, holds within his total wisdom and supreme initiation the entire sacred catalog of this planetary library.

He alone possesses in its entirety the cyclical key that is essential not only for opening each of its shelves, but also for knowing exactly what each of these shelves holds, for making one's way from one shelf to the next, and most importantly, for knowing how to get back out again.

Otherwise, what good would come to the profaner who has succeeded in forcing open one of the underground squares of this brain, this integral memory of humanity!

With all its dreadful weight, the stone door that seals each of these squares, lacking any kind of keyhole, will fall shut upon him, never to be opened again.

In vain, before realizing his terrible fate, he will find himself facing the mineral pages that make up this cosmic book, unable to spell even a single word of it, nor able to decipher the least of its mysteries before realizing that he has descended forever into a tomb from which his cries will never be heard by any visible being.

Each cardinal or Bagwandas, among the Powers that give him their seven hieratic names, possesses the secret of the seven celestial, terrestrial, and infernal regions, and has the power to enter and leave via the seven representational districts of this terrifying memorial of the Human Mind.

Ah! If Anarchy were not presiding over the relations of the peoples on earth, what a colossal renaissance would be achieved through all our religions and all our universities!

It is certain that our priests and admirable scholars, having entered back into the Universal Covenant of ancient times, would then perform their pilgrimages in Africa, in Asia, and in all the places where the tombs of a vanished civilization lie.

Not only would the earth surrender all of its secrets to them, but they would obtain a complete intelligence of it, the Dorian Key, and would return to our various institutions of learning to dispense not dead ash, but waves of living light.

But then, the past would no longer be profaned, and sepulchers no longer ravished of their relics, which are currently mutilated and thereby rendered inexplicable, and thence sent on to encumber our museums.

Antiquity would be piously rebuilt in its original locations: Egypt, Ethiopia, Chaldea, Syria, Armenia, Persia, Thrace, the Caucasus region, and even on the plateaus of Upper Tartary, where Swedenborg saw, through the ground, the lost books of the wars of Jehovah and the generations of Adam.

And then, the laureates of our highest studies would be led en masse to all these sacred resting spots of the human race, with Pontiffs and hymns at their heads!

Ah! Would that Science, rather than existing in our midst as the servant of governmental Anarchy, the slave of force, the instrument of ignorance and iniquity, and the public ruin of all our European nations, might instead rise up again, tiara on her forehead, cross in hand, and return to her ancient luminous peaks!

If, presiding anew over the relational life of the many peoples, she could finally achieve everything that all the prophets of every religion have predicted, what a divine concord would join back together all the bleeding limbs of Humanity!

This Humanity would no longer be a Christ on the cross over the entire planet, but a glorious Christ reflecting all the sacred rays of the Godhead, all the arts, all the sciences, all the splendors, and all the benefits of that divine Spirit who illuminated the past, and, through our painful gestations, endeavors once more to illuminate the future.

The public economy, freed of the horrific weight of armaments and taxes, will touch all that once was with its golden staff.

Then we would witness the rebirth of Ancient Egypt with its purified Mysteries, Greece in all the transfigured splendor of its Orphic Era, and a new Judea, more beautiful even than that of David and Solomon, and Chaldea before Nimrod.

Then everything would be renewed from top of human organization to the bottom; everything would be illuminated and known, from the heights of Heaven to the central furnace of the earth.

There are no intellectual, physical, or moral disorders to which the coming together of the teaching institutions and the positive reunion of Man with the Godhead would not provide a sure remedy.

The holy ways of the Generation would be discovered anew, the ways of sanctified Life, the ways of Death illuminated by ineffable consolations and worshipful certitudes; and the whole of Humanity will realize the words of the Prophet dazzled by the Mysteries of the other Life: Death, where is thy sting?

We must proceed toward this Synarchic era through the final bloody death agonies of the Anarchy of the general government inaugurated in Babylon.

This is my purpose for writing this book, and it is my intention to draw the reader even deeper into the sacred center of ancient Paradesa.

Following the alternating open and closed circles of the three hundred and sixty-five Bagwandas, come those of the twenty-two, or rather twenty-one, black and white Archis.

The difference between them and the highest initiates of the preceding circles is purely official and ceremonial.

The Bagwandas may choose to dwell in Agarttha or not as they please, but the Archis remain there forever as an integral part of its hierarchical heights.

Their duties are quite extensive, and they assume the Kabbalistic names of Chrinarshis, कृणार्ब्रि, Swadharshis, स्वधर्ब्रि, Dwijarshi, दिजर्ब्रि, Yogarshi, योगर्ब्रि, Maharshi, माहर्ब्रि, Rajarshi, रजर्ब्रि, Dharmashi, धर्मर्ब्रि, and finally Praharshi, प्रहर्ब्रि.

These names provide a sufficient indication of all their spiritual and administrative attributes in the sacred university, as well as all other areas in which they exercise their influence.

With respect to the arts and sciences, they form, in combination with the twelve Bagwandas of the Zodiac, the culminating point of the University teaching board and of the great alliance in God with all the cosmic powers.

Above them is only the triangle formed by the Sovereign Pontiff, the Brâhatmah, ब्राहत्मह्, meaning the support of souls in the Mind of God, and his two assessors, the Mahatma, माहत्म, representing the universal soul, and the Mahanga, माहाङ्ग, symbol of the complete physical organization of the Cosmos.

In the subterranean crypt where the body of the last Pontiff is laid to rest, where it waits the entire life of his successor before being incinerated in a sacred manner, we find the Archis who form the zero of the Mysteries represented by his twenty-one colleagues. His name Marshi means Prince of Death, and shows that he does not belong to the land of the living.

All of these different circles of degrees correspond to an equal number of circumferential or central portions of the Holy City, and remain invisible to those who walk on the Earth.

Thousands upon thousands of students have never penetrated past the first suburban circles; few manage to scale the rungs of Jacob's formidable ladder, which leads them through ordeals and initiatory exams into the central dome.

This last edifice, a work of magic architecture like all of Agarttha, is lit from above by catoptric scales, which allow the light* to arrive through the enharmonic spectrum of colors as opposed to the solar spectrum described in our books on physics, which is merely diatonic.

This is where the central hierarchy of the Cardinals and the Archis, arrayed in a semicircle before the Sovereign Pontiff, appears iridized as if seen from outside the Earth, commingling the shapes and appearances of the two Worlds, and drowning all visible distinctions of race in celestial radiances, in a single chromatic of light and sound, uniquely removed from the conventional notions of perspective and acoustics.

During the great prayer days, during the celebration of the cosmic Mysteries, although the sacred hierograms are recited in a tone little more than a whisper inside the immense underground dome, a strange acoustic phenomenon take place on the surface of the earth and in the skies.

The travelers and caravans that wander far during the light of day or on clear nights come to a halt, both man and beast, anxiously listening.

It seems to them that the Earth itself has opened its lips to sing.

---

*[From the planet's surface. —*Trans.*]

An immense harmony with no visible cause is in fact floating through space.

It unfolds in growing spirals and tenderly shakes the Atmosphere with its waves, then rises to be engulfed in the Heavens, as if seeking there for the Ineffable.

All that can be seen in the distance during the night is the trembling of the Moon and the Stars watching over the slumber of the mountains and valleys, while in the day all that is visible is the resplendence of the Sun over the most enchanting sites to be found on this Earth.

Whether Arabs or Parsis, Buddhists or Brahmanists, Karaite Jews or Subbas, Afghans, Tartars, or Chinese, all travelers respectfully gather their thoughts, listen in silence, and softly utter their orisons in the Great Universal Soul.

Such is the shape taken by the hierarchy of Paradesa from its base to its apex, a veritable pyramid of light enclosing the bond of an impenetrable secret.

At its culminating point, the reader will have already read the symbols of Synarchy in the sacred triangle formed by the Brâhatmah and his two assessors, the Mahatma and the Mahanga.

The authority residing in the divine spirit, the power in the judicial reason of the Universal Soul, and the economy in the physical organization of the Cosmos are all confirmation that the Trinitarian Law of history is located at the very head of the Ramid and Manavic corpus.

The instruction received by the adept, just after being accepted by the Divine Will that illuminates human wisdom, is still the same today as it was in the times of Ram and Menes.

This is because once the Synthetic Truth has been experienced, the progress of individuals consists of ascending to it in order to preserve it and propagate it unceasingly in the minds and souls of people.

Whether it be Moses or Orpheus, Solon or Pythagoras, Fo-Hi or

Zoroaster, Krishna or David, every applicant, every student, must begin
at the bottom rung before making his way to the top.

Newton or Lavoisier, Humboldt or Arago would either have to leave
or start over with the ABC's, yes the ABC's.

All Science in fact resides within the sacred Logos, from the most
infinitesimal part of the physical order to the most sublime aspect of
the divine order.

Everything speaks and everything has meaning, everything wears its
own name visibly written in its shape as a symbol of its nature, from
the insect to the Sun, from the subterranean fire that devours all matter
to the celestial fire that absorbs all essence back into its being.

What I am saying here must be taken literally as well as figuratively.

There is a universal Language of which the reader will catch some
fairly precise glimpses in my book *Mission of the Jews,* and this Language
is nothing other than the Logos of the first cycles about which Saint
John speaks:

בראשית חיה הדבר והדבר היה
עם האלהים ואלהים היה הדבר:

> *In the Principle was the Word*
> *(the power of creative Manifestation);*
> *and the Word was in Him the Gods;*
> *and in Him the Gods was the Word.*

Oh! How far we have wandered from this wise language, so simple
in all its principles and so certain in all its infinite applications.

Open any textbook of physics or chemistry, and you will see the dread-
fully incorrect names, the signs devoid of intrinsic meaning that compose
their nomenclature and express their equivalents and their laws.

In the ancient tongues, the same objects were described based on
their natures by absolute verbal symbols that evoked the true nature of
beings, of things, and their formation and decomposition.

So, brought back to their roots in the living Logos, the mathesis and morphology of the Dorian Logos were themselves a divine action that put everything in Nature, as Moses said, under the jurisdiction of human intelligence and science.

Inside their underground cells, the countless numbers of Dwijas spend their time studying all the sacred languages, and crown the works of the most amazing philology with wonderful discoveries of the universal Language about which I just spoke.

This Language is Vattan.

May the white haired in the company of those whose brows remain as yet unwrinkled spend their solitude absorbed in the study of these mysterious letters!

Each of these stone alveoli have been lit by means of oxydric gas since the remotest antiquity, a gas that cleanses the air rather than contaminates it like our hydrogen carbonate.

How many millions of Sages have emerged radiant from these granite tombs!

From the sons of Pontiffs or kings to the children of humble pariahs, what a selection of luminous souls has been crafted within these caverns.

Each of these grottos, however narrow it may be, has been skillfully aerated.

When in this solitude, the student can already feel his being invaded by the Invisible.

Little by little, holy visions will illuminate his slumber or his open eyes, rewarding his efforts toward Science and toward Virtue, or they will flog the indolence of his mind and his heart.

Living quarters similar to those of our marine officers serve the Dwija as sleeping chambers.

Every evening, he inflates his mattress and pillow with his own breath.

The only furniture is a table and chair. Several mysterious sentences are written on the walls: all calculated for producing inner concentration in the soul, without any distraction from outside.

When the study of the sacred languages has revealed the personal constitution of the divine Mind within the universal Soul, verification will begin through the four hierarchies of sciences, which I examined in great detail in *Mission of the Jews*.

Once the exams have been passed with honor, the Dwija gradually enters into the circles of years that will lead him to becoming a Yogi.

The first to open to him are all the degrees of the natural sciences, as they were taught in the underground cities of Egypt before the invasion of the Hyksos.

I will not repeat here what I have said elsewhere on this subject: everything taught by our secondary and higher institutions of learning, and everything that still remains for them to discover about physical nature, is taught here by teachers who have no rivals anywhere on earth; they are akin to Priests of Education.

The physiological constitution of the Planet and the cosmos are known down to their tiniest details, both physical and essential, both visible and invisible.

All things have been profoundly studied, from the igneous entrails of the Globe, to its underground rivers of gas, fresh water, and salt water; and even the living beings that inhabit these flames, these gases, or these waters.

All things have been profoundly studied, from the breadth and abyssal depths of the seas, to the role of the magnetic currents that connect one pole to the other in longitude and one tropic to the other in latitude.

All things have been profoundly studied, from matters concerning the air, including the invisible essences that dwell there, to the electricity that develops there, in echoes, after having been formed in the bowels of the earth, to where it will eventually return.

Aerial fleets of dirigible balloons have carried observations to a degree that is wholly inaccessible to our current methods.

Everything has been revealed, even the universal harmonies that produce the terrestrial seasons, the climbing migrations of souls through the North Pole, the elusive Mount Meru, and the indecipherable Alborj of the Vedic and Pehlevi books.

Electric railroads, made not of iron but of tempered and malleable glass, crisscross the ancient empire of Aries, without imprudently impoverishing the planet of its carbon reserves as is done today, nor burdening it with an iron armature that could not be any more lacking in foresight or any more favorable for the propagation of certain cosmic calamities.

And these sciences and these arts, and many others as well, continue to be ceaselessly professed, demonstrated, and practiced in the workshops, laboratories, and observatories of Agarttha.

Chemistry and physics have been developed to such a degree that no one would even want to accept my description, were I to depict them here.

We know naught but the forces of the Planet, at the most!

But despite these latter, the attractive Powers of the Heavens have been sacredly observed and continue to be the subject of ceaseless experiments.

What immense works, reaching down even to the infinitesimally small!

There is not an insect, not a plant, not a mineral, not even a drop of dew, whose dynamic properties have not been inventoried and made the subject of an incredible number of observations and experiments.

But there are yet more gigantic works in the realm of the infinitely large, not only on the physics of the Heavens (which we have not even begun to grasp), but on the physiology and sociology of the entire Universe!

No telescope could accomplish such a thing: thousands of souls, from one century to the next on up to the present, moved by an invincible faith and enlightened by absolute certitudes, have made the ascent into the Heavens, from Star to Star and from Sphere to Sphere, to arrive before the Flaming veil from which every spirit radiates and from which all life originates.

They have explored in every direction the celestial city about which every religion speaks.

And during this time, in the sacred crypts, the supreme council of Magi follows them, watching closely for the slightest sign emerging from the lips of these intrepid investigators, who lie stiff and cold as corpses.

Yes, here celestial Nature has surrendered and will continue to surrender her holy Mysteries.

With respect to the attractive forces of the Heavens, their effect on our purely physical forces has been and continues to be the subject of constant experimentation.

In a portion of their scientific Mysteries, the Magi of Agarttha are unable to approach certain subjects of study without being snatched up from the earth, as was the case with Apollonius of Tyana.

And those on whom, because of faith, the attractional powers of the Heavens are strongest, would break their skulls against the vault of the dome if their colleagues were not there to halt their ascent.

Thus all that is at play in the universe is the weight that chains their bodies to the center of the Earth.

But it is not only upon the living that countless experiments have been performed.

The dead have been injected with substances exercising a connecting effect, forming a median bond between them and the cosmic essence of their souls that have ascended into the Heavens.

The attraction of these souls has lifted up these cadavers to dizzying heights during the night, before the very eyes of the Sages of whom I speak, and will only let them come back down to earth during the day.

This kind of occurrence will be repeated before our own scientists and priests, once Synarchic understanding has been achieved.

Why not before?

Because Agarttha will not open its gates without a guarantee, and because in Europe, even in France itself, a complete legislative agenda is required for a sacred university of this kind to be founded and to perform its experiments without supervision and without outside interference.

All the Yogis and Munis know, in fact, that they are placing their very lives at stake when they enter into such sciences and arts.

Now, if someone starts yelling here about the impossibility of such sciences, I will answer that our Western experimenters are almost touching upon their positive reality.

Their empiricism is already brushing the frontiers of the true Magic; it has already reached the furthest frontier of physiology and psychurgy; it has already almost reached the intersection of the occurrences that concern the natural and human sciences with those that belong to cosmic and divine understandings.

European readers who have, closely or from a distance, followed the works of Charcot, Voisin, Demarquay, Girard-Teulon, Liégeois, and many other current scientific explorers, will be less surprised by reading all I have just said and all I have yet to say on the subject of the sciences and the magic experiments of Agarttha.

However, the scientists of this holy university metropolis would find that our own scientists are practicing black magic when they operate on the unconscious living being by means of any suggestion other than that of the Godhead and its Agents.

The means that produce hypnotism in the hands of our doctors are in fact artificial, as is this latter phenomenon; and they are hardly any more propitious for their subjects' physical and psychological health than they are for their saintliness.

The ideopsychic dispositions of the experimenters and their subjects require a great deal of development in order to arrive with certainty at the luminous series of observations of Agartthian magic.

I know that curiosity, no less scientific than legitimate, is the true motivation of our scientists.

But this is not enough to incline the invisible divinity to allow a glimpse of its Powers, nor the soul to feel them and, through its union with them, to surrender the secret of its dynamic faculties.

With respect to the subjects, their ignorance, their unhealthy state, their mental disturbance, their unawareness of what will be done to them and what is done at their expense, and their neurotic-psychic confusion, offer nothing but pathological conditions that are incompatible with the marvelous manifestations, which, throughout the whole of Antiquity, have proven to the scholars of the Sanctuaries the existence of the soul and the Deity.

Whatever form Western experiments may take, they shall not attain the Power of the Logos by empirical means; while the correlation of colors and mother vowels, sensed by those hypnotized by Monsieur de Liégeois, touches much more closely upon the greatest Mysteries.

I have described earlier how the bowels of the globe have been visited, and the infernal labors of their inhabitants observed there.

What once was still exists, and here is what the initiates of certain degrees say to those of others:

> Every year, at a predetermined cosmic time, under the guidance of the Maharshi and the high prince of the Sacred College of Magic, the laureates of the top sections descend once again to visit one of the Plutonian metropolises.
>
> They must first flow through the earth by way of a crack in the surface, which scarcely allows for the passage of a human body.
>
> Breathing comes to a halt, and the Yogi, his hands above his head, slips through it—an experience that feels as if it lasts a century.
>
> Eventually they all fall, one after another, down into an endless sloping gallery. This is where their true journey begins.
>
> As they descend, the air becomes increasingly impossible to breathe and, illuminated by the light from below, they can see

the force of the initiates increasing gradually along the length of immense inclined vaults, at the bottom of which they will soon catch sight of hell's fires.

The greater part of their number is forced to stop in the middle of their journey, suffocating and exhausted despite their provisions of breathable air, food, and calorific substances.

Only those continue who have become able, by the practice of secret arts and sciences, to breathe with their lungs as little as possible, and to use their other organs to draw from the air, in any given place, those divine and vital elements it contains wherever it is found.

Finally, after an extremely long journey, those who have persevered will witness something flaming in the distance that looks like an immense subplanetary conflagration.

The Initiatory Prince will turn around, and with his hand raised, thumb and index finger together, he will speak only through signs, in that universal Language about which I spoke earlier.

What does he say? Here it is:

"Silence! We have arrived. Speak not a word, touch neither the water nor any of the underground fruits of the people you are about to see; and when I cross the Ocean of fire, place your feet exactly in the prints my own have left."

In the same language, the Initiatory Prince will then face and address the beings that cannot yet be seen.

By the sacred hierograms, symbols of the Union of the celestial peoples with our Terrestrial humanity, symbols of the right of command that the divine Mind that animates this humanity has over what is below in the name of what dwells on high, the Prince of Magi commands, and the leaders of the infernal peoples obey.

The cyclopean metropolis opens, lit from below by a fluid red ocean that is a distant reflection of the central fire, which has withdrawn into itself during that time of the year.

There is an infinite array of the strangest kinds of architecture, in which all minerals commingled achieve what the fancies and chimeras of the Gothic, Corinthian, Dorian, and Ionian artists would never have dared dream.

And everywhere, furious at the sight of their home penetrated and invaded by men, a people of human shape and igneous bodies surge forth at the approach of the initiates and leap away on their wings in all directions to perch with their claws clinging to the plutonian walls of their city.

With the Maharshi at their head, the sacred procession follows a narrow path of basalt and hardened lava.

A dull noise can be heard in the distance that seems to extend infinitely, like the shudder caused by the waves of a great equinoctial tide.

During this time, while still moving forward, the Yogis observe and study these strange people, their mores, their customs, their frightening activity, and what use they might be for us.

It is their labors which, at the command of the Cosmic Powers, adapt to our benefit the layers of earth that support us, the underground rivers of metalloids and metals that are necessary to us, the volcanoes that guarantee explosions and cataclysms for our globe, and the systems of our mountains and river valleys.

It is also they who prepare the thunder, by damming up the cyclical currents of the interpolar and intertropical fluids beneath the earth's surface, as well as their interweaving derivations in the various zones of Earth's latitudes and longitudes.

It is also they who consume every living seed as it rots, so that it will be able to bear its fruit.

These people are the Autochthonous Inhabitants of the Central Fire; they are the same who were visited by Our Lord Jesus Christ before he ascended back into the Sun, ensuring that the Redemption would purify everything—even the igneous instincts from which the visible hierarchy of beings and things is erected here below.

This is because everything is life and everything is harmony in the mind of God, from the summit of the Heavens down into the very center of the Earth.

Here, the European reader, casting aside my book, will shout: "Do you really believe all this, really?"

Yes, sir, and here is the reason why.

What I have been privileged to learn and evaluate directly of the celestial Mysteries makes it impossible for me to doubt the reality of the infernal Mysteries, nor the veracity of any true initiate.

Furthermore, Agarttha is by no means the only Temple that has communicated with the depths of the globe.

All the Celtic priests and priestesses did the same, which earned druidic Europe the name of Empire of Pluto and Kingdom of the Amenti.

According to the esoteric tradition preserved through all the Temples and all Religions, there are no elements—by which I mean elementary states—that do not act under the influence of spiritual essences.

This is why, along with Saint Athanasius, Synarchic Catholic of the Universal Church, I say, with hands clasped: *Credo in unum Deum, Patrem omnipotentem, Creatorem Cæli et Terræ, Visibilium omnium et Invisibilium!*

[I believe in one God, the all-powerful Father, Creator of Heaven and Earth, of all that is Visible and Invisible!]

The esoteric doctrine of the Vedas consists of eight physical, cosmic, and divine elements, and consequently eight orders of spirits presiding over the organic constitution of these elements.

Bvumir, भूमीर्.

Apo, आपो.

Analo, अनलो.

Vâyus, वायु.

Hham, खम्.

Mano, मनो.
Buddir, बुद्दिर्.
Ahankara, अहङ्कर.

The same doctrine adds four cosmogonic powers:

Agnael, अग्नैल्.
Yamael, यमैल्.
Varanael, वरणैल्.
Uvael, उवैल्.

Under other names, the same powers are expressed in the text of Moses' Egyptian and Agartthian Cosmogony.

Is it possible for a conscious relationship to exist between Man and these Powers?

The Agartthian University still says yes today, and proves it through experiment.

Chapter Two

I will speak later about the immense consolations that Agarttha holds in reserve and that it will pass on to the scholars of the supreme Council of Teaching after the Synarchic Covenant.

There they will find all possible experimental demonstrations of the existence of the soul, both in the living being and after the cessation of physical life.

Here, I wish only to indicate the extent to which studies concerning this particular subject have been carried.

Among the formidable accumulation of experiments contained in Agarttha, those that concern human selection have been carried to an unprecedented degree.

Working in their own lands, independent and sure of their territories, the scientists of the Cycle of Aries have risked everything to gain an understanding both of the mystery of the species and the upper and lower limits of the physiological organization of humanity.

One of their ancient seminaries of selective breeding was situated on a group of seven islands, now vanished, that were once located in what our oceanographers call the Great Malabar Current.

These island dwelling people [an ancient traveler who lived among them for seven years informs us] are men who are very different from all others, as much in their mores as in the way they are built.

They are all more than six feet high and are all of the same build.

Their bones are quite elastic: these bones can bend and return to their original form like tendons.

Although their bodies may appear weak, their muscular system is infinitely stronger than our own.

It is impossible to take away anything they hold clenched in their fingers.

They have very handsome faces and are admirably proportioned.

Their ears, which are more open than our own, have double cavities that are separated by median strips of skin.

Their tongues have a strange quality that is partially artificial, due to a surgical operation: they are split from the tip to the root.

This anatomical configuration allows them not only to articulate all the sounds of every language in the world, but to imitate the songs and cries of all animal species.

But there is something about this that is most wondrous above all else: the same man, thanks to these two tongues, can converse with two people simultaneously and respond to them on completely different topics without confusing the two conversations.

This is something fundamentally no more astonishing than what our own pianists and organists are capable of doing with their two hands, and even their two feet.

They possess admirable hot water springs for bathing for pleasure or for hygiene.

There is not a science or an art of which they are unaware; but among them all, sacred astronomy is their preferred study.

They use seven letters in their writing; but each of these characters has four different positions, which brings the number of their letters to twenty-eight.

They do not write from left to right as we do, but vertically.

They live for a very long time; the ordinary life span of their old-timers is a century and a half.

During this long existence, only a rare few of them ever become ill.

When they have achieved this point of longevity, they voluntarily and consciously make the passage from life to death, by sleeping on a mattress made of particular herbs that gradually induce a delicious slumber from which they will never awake.

This, I think all will agree, is a lesson in physiological selection that shows what yet remains for us to discover and what it is possible to do in this domain.

The scientists of Agarttha are currently still capable of repeating these marvels.

But, in the seminaries of which I have been speaking, the science of selection does not stop with man, as the following will testify:

They have an animal species that are quite small, but that possess extraordinary physical capabilities.

Their backs, similar to those of turtles, bear a yellow cross in the form of an X, each end of which is lit by an eye and armed with a mouth.

The animal thus has four eyes that connect to a single brain, and four moths that provide access to a single stomach.

Their entrails and all their other internal parts are equally singular.

These animals are multipeds, and their means of locomotion, consisting of feet joined to the circumference of their bodies, allows them to move on all sides wherever their will leads them.

Their blood has the plasmatic property of immediately reconnecting and healing parts cut from a living body, such as the hand or foot, when the wound is recent.

I saw a great number of other kinds of animals, whose shapes are unknown to us and which have never been dreamt of in our imaginations.

These islands are filled with gigantic serpents that pose absolutely no danger of any kind, and whose flesh is quite succulent.

Although the dietary regime of these tribes is cleverly regulated, not everyone eats the same foods. Instead, depending on the days that are marked out for them, some must live on fish and others on poultry, some on olives and others on plant foods, while others live on raw fruits.

The preceding material, which I cited with express purpose, is the summary Diodorus provided of the voyage of Iambulus.

This traveler remained in the seminary for seven years, and he speaks of it with complete knowledge of the facts.

His account proves that even outside the temples, the ancient science of the Agartthians was by no means unknown.

The distinctive features of the selective breeding about which he speaks can leave no doubt as to its origin.

Furthermore, in certain regions of India, albeit only among the semi-savage descendents of former subjects of physiological experimentation, the same practices are still pursued empirically today.

The science and art of selection are admirably preserved in the stone libraries, and is a subject of constant study, along with the four hierarchies of Knowledge.

Within this sacred enclosure, there is not a single truth or a single tradition that is presented to the Dwijas without having been experimentally proven.

In addition to all we have just seen, experiments of all kinds teach the soul to know itself, and to comprehend itself anew in all the extent of its substance and its divine Kingdom, by means of the Science that leads to Wisdom, by means of the Will that gives Virtue, and by means of Prayer and Intimate Union with God and with his Powers that open the successive doors of the Heavens and their angelic Mysteries only to those that please them.

The ineffable agent, the sacred element that serves as flesh to the Eternal One and his divine faculties, is called Ether in all our languages, and is known as Akasha in Sanskrit.

Here, I refer the reader to everything I said on this subject in my earlier book, *Mission of the Jews.*

Ether is a living element that intoxicates one in an inexpressible manner with a sacred and entirely spiritual drunkenness, which the human intellect may nonetheless master sufficiently to preserve its individual reason and consciousness and maintain the body in a waking state—at the cost of very great effort.

It is then that the invisible becomes visible to our eyes.

Here people will ask me: "How is this done? Tell us, speak! What are the psychic or physiological means used to obtain this priceless benefit?"

God forbid that I should answer this question! For such a subject can be explained only within the Churches and Universities, and only once they have been reconciled.

In the meantime, ask the Saints of our Judeo-Christian Churches; and ask our priests how some of them, through their own spontaneity, inspired by divine love to the point of total self-renunciation, without art, without science, and without any visible guide, but with Jesus as their occult Hierophant, have received the visit of the Sacred Element that permeated them even to the marrow of their bones, and gave them bliss.

Ask also your holy women, from Saint Teresa to Joan of Arc, who are the most dazzling displays of divine manifestations in humanity since the appearance of the Savior.

Each and every one of them will answer you: It is Faith, it is Charity, it is Hope, it is Adoration to the point of absolute annihilation of oneself, to the point where the individual is entirely engulfed in the sentiment and sensation of human, celestial, and divine universality.

And they will be completely right to answer you in this way.

I will only add one more brief word.

Asceticism can lead to this truth, to this path, to this life of the blessed with psychic spontaneity fulfilling all the preceding conditions.

However, in Agarttha, asceticism is not practiced and will never be practiced as a rule of life in society.

It is reserved to individual freedom, when the Yogi wishes to retire from the world and, taking up residence in caves within virgin forests, returns absolutely to God by becoming a hermit or a Muni.

Ah! Saints are saints everywhere, in whatever form and through whatever religion they offer themselves in sacrifice to the living Spirit and to the eternal Christ, whom all revere under a thousand names!

Whether it be our own pious hermits of times past, or those of an entirely different communion, the Essenes or the Therapeutae,* the hermits of the Thebaid† or those of the Himalayan wilderness, I revere all of them in my faith as a Synarchic Christian, and I pray to all of them to deign to bless and protect my labors.

To those initiates who do not wish to follow the free path of monachism in the etymological sense of the word (*monos* meaning alone, which in Sanskrit is *Muni*), Agarttha nevertheless offers the possibility and practice of Divine Union, given a suitable dietary regime.

---

*[A group of ascetic philosophers described by Philo of Alexandria. —*Ed.*]
†[A historical region in the south of Egypt. —*Ed.*]

This is why, from the Dwija to the Brâhatmah, from the first of the initiates to the last, the peoples of this Cycle and this Communion in God abstain from all meat and all fermented liquor.

These conditions, combined with all those that Saintliness and Science command, will gradually bring the body into a state capable of allowing the Soul to regain possession of its celestial freedom.

In this way, for example, not only during waking, not only in complete trance, but even during the slumber of every night, High Initiation opens the whole of Heaven to its adepts.

The Epopt, in fact, no longer sleeps that merely animal slumber common to all the physical beings of the Earth.

In this mystery of sleep, whose existence has been suspected among us only by Boerhaave, the vital instinct that oppresses the soul becomes intoxicated by the ether of the lower domains, which we call terrestrial magnetism.

These well-known fluids of the ancient Orphic initiations are mentioned throughout the Egyptian Cosmogony of Moses.

A dietary regime based on meat and spirits, bringing man closer to the lower species, immerses his soul, during sleep, even more deeply in the aforementioned fluids.

If, under such conditions, the psychic force frees itself, it is because it feeds while one is awake upon other less material elements, under the instigation of the different orders of sentiment and ideality corresponding to the more or less elevated spheres of the Celestial Regions.

This is where the more or less luminous dreams of the young and old, of men and women, originate according to the degree of their ideopsychic release or that of their spiritualization.

Intelligence is in fact a celestial opening through which the universal Spirit enters and is assimilated by our souls, just as terrestrial substances are assimilated by our bodies.

The greater this assimilation, the more the soul that is becoming spiritualized will tend to reabsorb into itself the igneous instinct that it has received from the Earth, and which has bound it to physical existence.

But this universal Spirit, this Holy Spirit of our Christian faith, is not merely a mental abstraction within us.

It is living in Itself and by Itself.

Through the opening, It is granted by our intelligence, It does not merely work upon our intellectual faculties with Its celestial flame, but upon all the harmonic registers of our sentiments, for which Love is the central principle, identical to It.

After the long periods of training he must undergo in order to return in this way to the place of human-divine Life, the Epopt receives the secret of awakening while his body sleeps.

Wrapped in a shroud that covers his head and hermetically seals his ears, eyes, and nostrils, leaving only a space open for the mouth, with his arms crossed over his chest, he offers himself alive to the Angel of Death, and abandons all power to abnegate his will completely to God.

And, following prayers made in mysterious Words, seized by the Angel of Death, the soul is lifted up into God through the Hierarchy of Angels while the body remains lying like any other sleeping man.

What does he see then? A dazzling light, and angels will take him wherever his piety and desire to learn are in accordance with the will of the Eternal One.

Thus, the bards of all the temples and of all times have been rightly able to say: The Sun never sets for him who by Initiation has returned into the Kingdom of God.

But each night, when he surrenders to the Angel of Death, there is no initiate who is sure of his physical reawakening and his life on earth the following day.

Ah, it is certainly no game that this colossal scientific reserve is playing by authorizing, motivating, explaining, and experimentally demonstrating the solid basis and logic of divine activity through all these means of social culture so rightly called religions.

By religions, I mean the great periodically occurring syntheses that, under the impetus of a sovereign Epopt such as Moses or a divine initiator such as Jesus Christ, redirect the perfectible members of the human race toward the perfect harmony from which our governments have forced them to stray.

No, it is certainly no game that the sciences and arts are playing by providing empirical evidence of this harmony of truths and realities, extending from the summit of the Heavens down into the very bowels of the Earth.

No, this is no game, where ancient Wisdom, faithful to itself, can still aid us to verify through experiments everything that Moses, Orpheus, the Prophets, and our divine Messiah were able to achieve.

But woe to those who, without absolute purity of intelligence, sentiment, and instinct, and without the supervision of Sacred Science, attempt to force the doors of Eternity!

Woe to those who, outside Wisdom and Holiness, would attempt to leap from the other side of things, with heads lowered, into the Ocean of resplendent Ether!

Woe finally to those imprudent folk who surrender the positive keys of the Occult to nations or individuals who have not been sufficiently prepared to receive them, and outside of the channels of Religion, Teaching, and Initiation, divinely designed and preserved for this purpose!

Although they have been brushed by the Ether, these Promethean profaners will fall as if struck by lightning into the abysses of the Ahankara, the element of the individual ego and the instinctive life, burned down to their bones, not by the tongues of flame of the celestial Spirit but by all the fires of genital concupiscence.

For the same celestial fire that inhales pure souls and sucks them into the Spirit on high, spits the impure down into the igneous forces of the Earth; and while the former are with the Angels, blissfully enjoying celestial love, the others ride astride demons and are swallowed up in the gulfs of the infernal orgy.

— —

This is the reason why, outside the great moral enclosure of Judeo-Christianity, and outside the Church of the Primordial Ones known as Agarttha, the schism of Irshu has come to pass everywhere: in Assyria, in Syria, in Egypt under the Hyksos, and throughout the whole of European Ionia. In these places the idolatry of poorly understood cosmic powers, combined with the adulterated knowledge of the mysteries, has paraded the torch of the orgiastic Sabbaths from the Ganges to the Nile, from the Euphrates to the Eurotas,* from the Kithairon mountains† to the seven hills of Rome.

This is also why these terrible profanations have earned such terrible punishments.

They have not ceased at this time in which I am speaking, and even in India, wherever the direct influence of Agarttha is not felt, the same disorders are more or less being reproduced.

Ah! Let us all beat our chests, in the presence of the plagues of humanity, and from one end of Earth to the other, let us all say together: It is our transgression, it is our transgression, it is our very greatest transgression!

Not a single temple, nor church, nor synagogue, nor mosque can hide from this universal linkage of men either in Evil or in Good.

"Pray unto me," the Eternal One tells them, "and give unto me your sacrifices! What I ask of you is to work toward your general Salvation by joining together through mutual charity in one common redemptive action."

No form of worship nor any teaching body, Agarttha no more than any other, can hide away with impunity henceforth from this great and holy solidarity.

No one can truthfully say: I wash my hands of this evil.

Any and all are, and will fatally be, subjects of the general Government of ignorance, iniquity, and the common ruin of nations,

---

*[River in the Peloponnese of Southern Greece. —*Trans.*]
†[In Central Greece. —*Trans.*]

just as the limbs of the social Christ, thanks to this abstention, will bleed or rot on its great equatorial and polar cross.

Alas! Still today, as in the times of Astarte and Aphrodite, of Eleusinian Ceres, Isis, and the false Bacchus of the decadent period, in certain pagodas of India where the priesthood is hereditary and not won through Examination as is the case in Agarttha, infamous things will still take place at certain times of the year.

I know it to be so, and no human power can prevent me from shouting it here, and cursing it for the scourge that it is.

And yet for you, initiates, who today as in times past, behind the sacred pylons, coolly watch these demoniacal bacchanalia take place, it is not enough to simply refrain from taking part. One must prevent them: it is the price to be paid for the resurrection and redemption of your country.

But now, let us return to Agarttha.

The absolute purity of its tradition, its teachings, its disciplines, and its morals has been vaguely sensed in every era.

As early as 1784, Herder himself, without suspecting its actual existence, stated that only the most learned and the most holy school would have been capable, throughout all Antiquity, of educating such a people as the Hindus, who, except in certain parts of Hindustan where the mysteries have deviated and where the law of Manu is no longer understood for want of being studied, generally offer an immense amount of divine and human virtues, which have never been developed to a greater extent anywhere else.

So, in order to avoid committing an injustice, it is necessary to gain a precise view of the very large number of sects that the various provinces of India offer for observation to the traveler.

There can be no doubt that their common root is the great University of which I spoke earlier, albeit in a time of the remotest Antiquity.

It would also be iniquitous to condemn this University for the shameful acts, superstitions, and atrocities engendered over the years by Anarchy, both local and general, and by the succession of conquests alternating with revolutions that has reduced the clerical establishment to servitude and caused the vices of political power to connive with the corruption of popular ideas and mores.

All idolatry stems from this, which is to say from Politics, the great Prostitute of Babylon as the Judeo-Christian prophets called it.

There is only one thing that should be cause for surprise: the fact that after a lifespan that can be measured in cycles, and despite all the evils unleashed by the schism of Irshu, India still exists and is still able to hold the immense amount of virtues that are ceaselessly cultivated there, as well as all the different kinds of knowledge that can be found in Agarttha.

Never under similar conditions, given the current political foundations, could Judeo-Christianity have been able to maintain itself and survive for five hundred years, much less five thousand.

And the barbarians of the *Carrières d'Amérique** of all our large cities have committed no fewer atrocities than certain branches of Shivaism, such as the Thuggee[†] or the worshippers of Kali.

Can one condemn the pure white peaks of the Himalayas, their virgin glaciers, their eternal snows, their uncontaminated springs, their proud limpid torrents, for the filth and corpses that tumble toward the sea on the troubled currents of the Indus or upon the tumultuous waves of the Ganges?

The same holds true for Agarttha, which has always expelled from its breast any intellectual or moral impurity as well as all intolerance, politics, any arbitrary stance of thought or will, all superstition, all idolatry, and all black magic.

---

*[A network of tunnels and quarries that existed under an area of northeast Paris, notorious for their vagrant population until they were filled in during the mid-nineteenth century. —*Ed.*]

[†][A group of professional criminals historically active in India; origin of the word *thug*. —*Ed.*]

This is the reason why various domestic duties of Agarttha have been shared for many centuries by the students and by weekly brigades under the supervision of the Templars, who provide all military and police duties.

This was not the case before Çakya Muni, when entire populations of subalterns took care of the cells of the Dwijas, the dwellings of the Pundits, and the laboratories and observatories of the University.

Here is the origin of this change from which the creation of a large number of sects can be dated, some of them more or less innocent, others more or less ferocious:

When the Buddhist schism erupted in the outside world, a kind of political revolution took place among the salaried servants of the university Metropolis.

Aware of their strength in numbers, they sought to overturn the Hierarchy of masters and authorities, in order to enthrone on its remains a fine little anarchy designed to their liking.

The sweepers of the chambers of philosophy dared to preach against the Mysteries and especially against the conditions of Initiation.

The laborers in the workshops, the laboratories, and the observatories now claimed to be doctors and immediately began practicing magic. They inevitably fell into black magic and, with the help of certain crippled formulas, received from below some responses to the decrees they purported to dictate from above.

It was at this time that the mass expulsion took place that gave birth to all the different tribes, some fixed and others nomadic.

Among the first, there was one that covered India with more blood than was ever spilled on the altars of Moloch, or on the racks of the Inquisition, or by the guillotines of 1793.

A monstrous heap of ignorance and superstition, commingling Brahmanists and Buddhists in the same hatred, this sect sculpted an enormous stone statue in certain gorges of the Himalayas.

Its lower jaw was mobile and opened a mouth that was several meters in circumference over an internal conduit that led to water-filled abysses.

A hydraulic mechanism caused the mandible of this gulf to move. Its constructors were the members of this atrocious priesthood.

These Shivaists restored the blackest and most infamous policies of druidic times, gradually accustoming the populace to the sacrifices they contemplated making, by causing their infernal deity to swallow entire herds of cattle alive.

In the distance a kind of subterranean thunder could be heard, a tempest of bellowing within the depths of the monster, that mingled with the horrific gurgling of water, the noise of chains, and the uninterrupted fracas of the infernal machine.

And the brutal idiots who ministered to the belly of this Brute, half mountain and half machine, declared their God to be satisfied—until the next day.

Soon, alas, it was the turn of any men—especially the most learned among them—on whom they could lay their hands.

And it went on like this for entire centuries!

Today it has been a long time since the jaw of that monster last functioned and the hydraulic machine that caused it to move stopped being used; but the sect still exists, using the dagger to do its work, however weakened and undermined it may have been throughout by the influence of Agarttha.

Among the less guilty of the tribes expelled from the great university, at the same time as those described above, there is a nomadic group that has been displaying its distinctive practices across Europe since the fifteenth century.

This group is, in fact, the true origin of the Bohemians. Their name is Bohami, बोहमि, which means *go away from me*.

These poor folk have carried with them some vague memories and a few spells buried in a heap of more or less vulgar superstition.

Sooner or later they will return to their native land once the Synarchic breath has restored to India the ancient spirit of its primordial, true, just, and good organization.

I cannot speak of these people expelled from Agarttha without saying a word about its most humble faithful who dedicate their lives to crisscrossing the whole of India and enchanting it with amazing miracles and marvelous works of poetry that are full of mystery.

Everyone has read about the extraordinary things the Fakirs are able to do.

Nary a traveler is to be found who has failed to speak of their feats, sometimes with enthusiastic admiration, but always with profound amazement.

The Fakirs are most often former students of Agarttha who stopped their studies at the entrance to the high degrees and dedicated themselves to a religious life, similar to the mendicant monks of our own Middle Ages.

Their sciences, or arts rather, are but mere morsels from the sacred table of esoteric teaching.

The secrets that the gurus of the university gave them are quite real; and the purpose of their humble mission is to carry into the least of aldéas* several phenomenological rays, proving to the Hindus that the ancient Science still preserves its luminous hearth somewhere.

I will not recall here the feats of all kinds with which these humble religious men confound the imagination.

The primary cause for the majority of these phenomena is the celestial force we call Ether.

The fakir, before performing his trick, is charged with ether in the temples as if he were a veritable human electric battery.

This operation is carried out as methodically as any of our experiments in physics or chemistry, although this order of phenomena

---

*[*Aldea* is a Portuguese word for small villages or villas that still survive in India from the era when Portugal had a colony in Goa. —*Trans.*]

simultaneously straddles the human sciences and, to a certain extent, those that involve the entire Cosmos.

Among the chemical agents that allow the fakirs to become, for a certain period of time, condensers saturated with Ether and terrestrial magnetism, there is one that is perfectly familiar to our laboratories but without anyone possessing a clue as to its occult and physiological-dynamic properties.

During his trance, all the fakir's physical extremities are coated with this substance and he becomes a veritable living torch, burning with a double fire that is etherized at the top and magnetized at the bottom.

These poor folk require a terrible faith, will, and abnegation to solicit and happily accept such a vital combustion.

Almost all of them die young; but in consolation they know they have achieved a mission vis-à-vis the most underprivileged of their compatriots, and have personally experienced the immense bliss of the uninterrupted Ocean of indescribable visions, from the heart of which they draw the forces whose presence is made evident on their exteriors.

I know that Agarttha, which has long been troubled by the decadence of certain branches of the official, hereditary priesthood in the southern provinces, as well as by the corruption of morals and the abuses that reign in the pagodas of the various sects, is doing its utmost to restore everywhere the scientific study of the sacred texts: the Vedas, the Zend Avesta, and the Hebrew text of Moses and the New Testament.

I know that a large number of high initiates have generously embraced the party of active reform, and that the Brâhatmah is silently awaiting the results of their efforts.

His pontifical duty as head of a sacred university does not permit him to do anything more, and forbids him from imposing on anyone those teachings and virtues that initiation renders unto those who know to ask for them.

The holy cause for this reform, which is nothing other than a return to the true sacred tradition of the Vedas, already includes among its numbers not only apostles but martyrs who have fallen riddled with the blows of daggers.

The Agartthians do not weep for these martyrs, for they know they are alive, and they envy them.

In fact, immortality of the soul in their teaching is not only a faith based on feeling, but is also an absolute certitude bequeathed by Knowledge.

Since the most distant Antiquity, every initiate, after dying, has been interrogated by the priest-scientists within a certain period that they have established.

The doors are sealed, the corpse lies upon the stone floor, and the soul that is flying off is summoned, by methods that are indicated in our own Holy Testaments and developed completely in the true text of the Vedas.

The soul describes, in the universal language, all the impressions it has felt starting from the moment when the Angel of Death carried it away, all the sensations it experienced after being swallowed by the fluidic Ocean, upon which the Sun during the day and the Moon during the night exercise their mysterious influences, in conjunction with the Stars.

The soul describes the attractive regions for which its spiritual leaders have prepared it according to its merits, either on high or down below, when the hour of the great migration of the human essences will have appeared on the sidereal dial of the Worlds.

It tells of the journeys of souls, those countless pilgrimages toward the North Pole and the infinite abductions and soaring flights, rising by the million into certain fluidic currents toward a neighboring star.

The soul then blesses those who remain and soars away, but without abandoning them.

Thanks to those substances I mentioned earlier, it has been possible to follow the Souls for a long time through all the ascending degrees of the Worlds, to the extreme limits that form the confines of our Solar System and open onto the Gan-bi-heden of the Egyptian cosmogony of Moses, the personal abode of Adam-Eve over which extend the Tabernacles of IÊVÊ, for which Christ is the solar mirror.

The kin of the dead are therefore able to draw ineffable consolations from these Sanctuaries; they know where their beloveds are and what they might find pleasant and useful. At certain cosmic times of the year they can see them and speak with them.

This is one of the secrets of the age-old worship of the ancestors. For more on this subject, I refer my reader to *Mission of the Jews,* in which I discuss the ancient Egyptian Book of the Dead.

There is so much more I could say! But it will be the duty of a body of scholars, once reconciled, rather than a single man, to reveal everything about these holy matters.

Is there any need to add that among all the sciences and arts, those of Prophecy are admirably taught and practiced in Agarttha?

These practices bear no resemblance whatsoever to what the Babylonian schism has left as its legacy to the curious of our time.

The Principles are in their rightful place, and the direct supervision of the Holy Ghost is perpetually invoked.

As in the most splendid days of Egypt and the ancient Synarchy of Aries and the Lamb, the feminine faculty enjoys all the same initiatory prerogatives as the masculine faculty.

The wife of every initiate can also become his equal in all the Divine Mysteries, and even surpass him, because their university and social rights are the same.

Christianity has thus been correct and faithful to the esoteric tradition of Moses, the Abramites, and the Ramids in granting to the divine mother of Christ all the prerogatives of the Isis of modern times.

It was in fact an Epopt who, in the Temple of Jerusalem itself, possessed, like Alma, all the secrets of esoteric science, all the holy virtues that called upon her to receive from the Deity and his Angels the dazzling soul of the Redeemer.

For any reader capable of reading between the lines, I have spoken of many things in my *Mission of the Jews* concerning the universities of Antiquity and the Ionian and Dorian Schools of the Prophetesses and Prophets, and there is no need to repeat them here.

I will confine myself to absolutely confirming everything that I have revealed or implied concerning these mysteries of the human mind and human life, from the time of the Cycle of Ram to that of the Temples of Egypt, from the age of Thrace, Etruria, and Sinai to that of Bethlehem and Calvary.

When the initiate has attained a certain degree, binding his soul to the divine Union and to the celestial Yogina, he is led into the caverns where he is shown a statue modeled after him, about which there can be no doubt. The statue is cast in an artificial mineral substance, like the obelisks of Egypt, over time acquiring a permanent durability.

Then, through the thousand branching paths of the radiant vaults, he sees an infinite number of statues of people.

His guide, whose head is adorned, depending on the time of the year, with this or that sign of the zodiac, softly whispers in his ear the name of each one of them.

All the Epopts of Humanity are there, all its benefactors and all its revealers, with no distinction of Worship or Race.

Something that can be seen here or there, but rarely, is a mutilated pedestal on which stands a broken shape, the debris of its limbs or head strewn across the floor.

This is an Epopt who has fallen and done evil to his fellows.

No initiate can take away with him from Agarttha the original texts of the books he has studied. They are, as I've said earlier, carved on stone in characters that are indecipherable to the common people.

Memory alone must allow him to preserve their image. This is what drove Plato, somewhere or other, to voice this bizarre paradox: Science was lost on the day someone first published a book.

In certain cases, a person is not even allowed to take his own manuscripts with him.

This was the reason why Çakya Muni, returning from an excursion to the outside world in the sixth century BC, gave a dreadful howl when he could not find the study books where he had left them in his cell.

He felt momentarily lost, counting upon this treasure to achieve the revolutionary movement that he had prepared in silence.

In vain did he rush to the central Temple where the Brâhatmah dwelt: its doors remained pitilessly closed.

In vain did he spend a whole night putting into operation everything the Science had taught him of Magic: the Divinatory power of the supreme sanctuary had foreseen all, and knew all.

Thus after his flight, the founder of Buddhism could only dictate to his disciples, in great haste, what his memory had been capable of retaining.

These words would be heard by the Buddhists and taken by them to the top of their hierarchy, all the way to the Parivena of Colombo, up to the Pontiff Sumangala.

My purpose in making all this known is to bring about everywhere the mutual covenant of the temples. The Buddhists were divulgers of great merit and virtue, and the Brahmans of Agarttha remain their true hierophants.

As I just said, before his final flight, the venerable Çakya Muni was unable to open the doors of the central sanctuary where dwelt the Brâhatmah.

Its walls, in fact, cannot be breached without his permission.

The cellar of this edifice is magically constructed by various means, in which the Divine Logos plays a role, as was the case in all the temples of Antiquity.

Except for Man and the attractive and intelligent powers of the Heavens, no earthly being can live there, nor can any seed of plant or animal be preserved there.

Let us enter this Tabernacle; there we shall see the Brâhatmah, proto-type of the Abramites of Chaldea, the Melchizedek priests of Salem, and the Hierophants of Thebes and Memphis, as well as of Saïs and Ammon.

With the exception of the highest initiates, no one has ever come face to face with the Sovereign Pontiff of Agarttha.

However, in certain well-known ceremonies, that of Jaggrenat for example, he appears before the eyes of all in his splendid vestments.

Mounted on his white elephant, he is all awash from his tiara to his feet in a dazzling light that blinds all eyes, with similar sparkling lights surrounding him.

But it is impossible to distinguish his features from those of the other pontiffs, for a fringe of diamonds reflecting all the fires of the sun veils his face in living flame.

These wise precautionary measures date from the rupture of the ancient Synarchy by the revolution of Irshu and were then given new impetus after Çakya Muni.

The ceremonial costume of the Brâhatmah sums up all the symbols of the Agartthian organization and the magic Synthesis founded upon the eternal Logos, of which it is the living image.

This is why all his garments, even his belt, bear the groups of all the magical letters that are the elements of the great science of the Aum.

The breastplate he wears over his chest blazes with all the fires of the symbolic stones, consecrated to the celestial intelligences of the Zodiac. The Pontiff is able to repeat at will the miracle of spontaneously light-ing the sacred flame on the altar, as did Aaron and his successors.

His seven-crowned tiara, surmounted by holy hieroglyphs, expresses the seven degrees of the descent and return ascent of the souls through those divine Splendors that the Kabbalists call the Sephiroth.

But this high priest appears even greater to me when, stripped of his insignia, he enters alone into the sacred crypt where the tomb of his predecessor lies. He then separates himself from all ceremonial pomp, removes every ornament, every bit of metal, and every jewel, and offers himself to the Angel of Death clad in naught but his absolute humility.

What a strange and terrible theurgical mystery!

The tomb of the preceding Brâhatmah is there, topped by a catafalque whose fringes indicate the number of centuries and the number of Pontiffs who have passed on.

Onto this funeral dais, upon which are lying certain tools of sacred magic, the Brâhatmah slowly climbs while intoning the prayers and making the gestures of his ancient ritual.

It was an old man of the Caucasian type, descended from this handsome Ethiopian race, who—after the Red and before the White—formerly held the scepter of the general government of the Earth, and carved in all the mountains those cities and prodigious buildings that can be found everywhere from Ethiopia to Egypt and from India to the Caucasus.

We find the Brâhatmah, completely clean shaven, in this funeral crypt in which none but he can enter. He is naked from his head to his waist; this humble nudity is the magic symbol of Death.

An ascetic, his body so elegantly jointed is nevertheless solidly muscled.

Three thin symbolic strips stand out at the top of his arms.

And above the string of beads and white scarf, which stands out sharply against the brilliant black of his body and falls from his shoulders to his knees, emerges a head possessing the most remarkable characteristics.

The features of his face are of an extreme finesse.

Although his teeth appear somewhat clenched from his habitually great concentration of intelligence and will, his mouth displays welcoming lips from which drifts the interior radiance of an unfailing charity.

His chin is small, but juts out sufficiently to indicate great energy, something also confirmed by his aquiline nose.

His eyeglasses permit a glimpse of well-defined eyes that are both fixed and deep, as well as good.

But these latter, which generally give every physiognomy a harder cast, here gives this one a nature of great tenderness combined with true authority.

His forehead is enormous, the top of his head slightly bald.

Out of all these Magus-Pontiffs emerges a type of being that is absolutely exceptional.

This being is clearly the living emblem of the summit of a hierarchy that simultaneously consists of the priesthood and the university, thus indivisibly combining within itself Science and Religion.

During this time that he is entirely concentrated upon the holiness of his inner activity and absolute will, the Pontiff joins together his hands, which are noteworthy for how small they are. At this same time the coffin of his predecessor has slid into a groove at the base of the catafalque and goes away as if self-propelled.

While the Brâhatmah continues his magic prayers, the soul he is invoking takes action in the heights of heaven through seven blades, or rather seven metallic conduits that, emerging from the embalmed body, combine before the Pontiff of the Magi in two vertical tubes.

One of these tubes is gold and the other is silver. The first of them corresponds to the Sun, to Christ, and to the Archangel Michael while the second corresponds to the Moon, to Mohammed, and to the Angel Gabriel.

His sacred staffs are placed somewhat further away and in front of the Sovereign Pontiff, and after them, two symbolic objects. One of these is a golden pomegranate, the emblem of Judeo-Christianity, the other a silver crescent, the symbol of Islam.

This is because Prayer in Agarttha unites in one love and in one wisdom all the religions that prepare within humanity the conditions necessary for its cyclical return to the Divine Law governing its organization.

When the Brâhatmah makes this prayer for the Union, he places the Pomegranate upon the Crescent, and simultaneously invokes the Solar Angel Michael and the Lunar Angel Gabriel.

While the Brâhatmah is continuing his mysterious invocations, the Powers appear before his eyes.

He feels and hears the soul he has summoned, which has been spiritually drawn to him by his invocations, magically attracted by the body it has left and by its metallic armature that corresponds to the diatonic scale of the seven Heavens.

Then, in the universal language of which I have spoken, a theurgical conference is initiated between the evocative Sovereign Pontiff and the Angels who carry down to him from on high the responses given to his requests.

Sacred signs trace in the air the absolute letters of the Logos.

While these Mysteries are being completed, while the music of the celestial Spheres makes itself heard, a phenomenon that is no less strange, albeit semimaterial, rises out of the tomb.

Out of the embalmed body a kind of perfumed lava slowly rises toward the praying Brâhatmah. Out of this lava sprout countless filaments and strange arborescences, half fluid and half tangible.

This is the sign that the soul of the previous Pontiff, from within the remote star he inhabits, is sending at full speed the concentrated rays of all his memories, through the Hierarchy of the Heavens and their celestial powers, toward the sacred crypt in which his body lies.

Thus, even at the present hour, all that Ram predicted concerning the successive animation that all his successors would receive from him is verified; and thus, in holiness and wisdom, they preserve the Tradition of the Cycle of the Lamb and the Synarchy of Aries.

Such is the supreme Mystery of ancestor worship in Agarttha, and so it was in the pyramids of Egypt, in Crete, in Thrace, and even in the druidic temple of Isis in Paris itself, where Notre-Dame now stands.

This is also the reason why all the esoteric initiators have always taken great pains to conceal their sepulchers from profanation.

There are only a few individuals among the high initiates themselves who know what I have just said about the Mystery of Funeral Crypt, which is solely guarded by the Archi from beyond the grave who bears the name of Marshis, the Prince of Death.

The Brâhatmah is married and has many offspring; but as I said in *Mission of the Jews,* heredity has no role to play in the true Ramid organization of Antiquity.

Even the sons or daughters of the Sovereign Pontiff himself cannot obtain any rank within the Agartthian hierarchy except by passing through the common law of the Examination.

This reduces to naught all the accusations of ignorance hurled against true Antiquity.

What our Pyrrhonians have taken everywhere for Theocracy was only the decadence of local priestly establishments under the pressure of the political powers created by the schism of Irshu.

Wherever independence has prevailed over any arbitrary form of constraint, permitting the ancient teaching authority to conserve its magisterial nature, we can see this latter reemerging even in our own day as the inevitable crowning moment of all social progress.

If these critics have cast blame upon the subservience of the priesthood, and of all manner of teaching bodies, to political authorities that offer compensations, offices, and honors, then they have been absolutely correct, and I am in complete agreement with them on this point.

But if they claim to infer from this that all teaching bodies, whose authority strictly speaking constitutes the social Theocracy, should remain in this subordinate position toward these same political authorities, then they are sadly mistaken and my duty is not to fight them but to enlighten them.

This is why, following my preceding *Missions,* I am revealing to them the most ancient University of the Globe, unveiled and in all its theocratic purity, a university consisting of some fifteen million people, not to mention an equally formidable number of affiliates.

May Europeans pay great heed to what I am about to say.

In my earlier *Missions,* I pointed out to them how mistaken it was to view China as a negligible quantity in the balance of powers of the Earth.

Two years before the last war, I spoke of how its armaments, its European military instructors, and its slow but certain evolution toward a war footing following probable State loans, would sooner or later transform it into a formidable adversary for Europe.

What I said then has already been partially realized, including the State loan taken out in London.

After having forewarned all our nations of the authority, both physical and rational, that they would have to take into consideration, namely the Power of the Celestial Empire, I am continuing my work in this *Mission of India in Europe, and Mission of Europe in Asia.**

But this time it is no longer a semiphysical and semibrutal supervising authority that is involved, it is the preeminently great intellectual and universitarian supervising authority whose existence I am revealing here along with its value, sovereignty, and moral authority in Asia.

> *Religions, open your ears!*
> *Nations, open your eyes!*
> *Judeo-Christian Europe, listen and try to understand!*
> *What is the Spirit of this august supervising authority?*

It is that of the ancient Kingdom of God, the same toward which the Abramites, Moses, and Jesus Christ guided us.

This Spirit is still that of the universal Covenant of all the members of humanity, that of the indissoluble Union of science and religion in all their universality.

In its love, faith, and hope, it embraces all accessible Divinity and all perfectible Humanity.

Since the time of the Abramites, not content with sending every-

---

*[The original French title of the present work. —*Ed.*]

where the Torchbearers, Epopts, and Prophets who in every direction
have combated through good deeds the social plagues that have been
unleashed upon the earth by the anarchy of political men, Agarttha has
continued to send into all nations immense human channels, who are
comparable to its underground libraries.

And just as Agarttha was the initiator of the Abramites, it was again
this underground realm that has renewed everywhere, at the beginning of modern times and through the work of the Judeo-Christian
Kabbalists, the thousands of associations being developed today under
the name of Freemasonry.

For more than a century in Europe, the unleashing of the physical
sciences has temporarily drowned the highest faculties of the human
mind, its synthetic or religious sense, and its most profound remem-
brances, in a deluge of valuable facts but incorrect nomenclatures.

Also since this time, the line of communication between Agarttha
and the West has been momentarily cut, because, let me repeat it one
more time, the name of this great university is: Closed to Anarchy!

Europeans, restore communication, believe me, not in an occult way
but out in the full light of day.

Through your religions, through your universities, through your
Masonic Lodges all finally reconciled, join together all your faculties,
combine your collective understanding, and meditate seriously upon
my *Missions* that are the surest grounds, and the physical and practical means for forming an essential alliance with all of Asia, which you
believe you know, and yet you know not.

I have sounded to the bottom before you the most hidden Mysteries
of its heart and of its thought, the incommensurable intellectual and
material treasures that its unyielding fidelity to Tradition holds in
reserve.

This study is profoundly edifying and consoling for whoever loves
humanity; but the situation is quite serious for you, O European nations,
and for anyone who has a profound understanding, as I do, of all the

mysteries of the mutual hatreds of your religions, your teachings, your classes, and finally of your nations infernally armed by science for your reciprocal destruction.

If you do not create Synarchy, I foresee a century of decline that will forever eclipse your Judeo-Christian civilization and will witness your brutal supremacy crushed once and for all by an incredible rebirth of the whole of Asia, an Asia resurrected, standing tall, a scholarly and believing Asia armed from head to toe that will achieve without you and in spite of you the social promises made by the Abramites, Moses, Jesus Christ, and all the Judeo-Christian Kabbalists.

And just as I am pointing out the danger you are incurring, I am shouting and will continue to shout its remedy so long as God gives me strength.

This remedy is not military in nature, for by attacking close to a billion Asians, you will end up merely providing them with military training, and sooner or later they will let you know their true strength.

Nor is this remedy diplomatic: almost all of Asia is already part of your diplomatic corps and, caught in the gears of the machine of your mutual jealousies and ruses, they will in turn entrap you in these same gears one day and break you between them and the two Americas.

The remedy I am offering to you is one that your sacred books, your social sciences, and universal History holds in hand, and it is a purely intellectual, judicial, and organic solution.

This remedy is Synarchy, the historic law of humanity that I have demonstrated irrefutably in my previous works.

It is here and nowhere else that your salvation lies, both with respect to yourselves and to Asia.

It is here that any possible understanding with them lies, any meeting of minds and wills, and it will depend on your own educational, economic, and judicial bodies, in other words all your priests and all your teachers, all your governments and all your productive capabilities.

If this same European general government, scorning my warnings that are the very same as those given by Christ, demands protection from violence and aggression that can only be had from the Synarchic spirit of Judeo-Christianity, it will certainly also hasten the moment when a torrent of human catastrophes will be unleashed upon it and upon our nations, despite the efforts of Agarttha itself, the born enemy of all violence.

And so I cry to all of them, in the name of God: Synarchy, Synarchy, Synarchy!

This is how you can save your tiaras and your miters, your churches and your universities, your crowns and your republics, and everything that is properly your own, everything, including whatever was legitimate in the Revolution of '89* with regard to its social promises—promises that only Judeo-Christian Synarchy can hold and fulfill.

Unite together in this Law, ecclesiastical and secular teaching bodies, economic bodies, and judicial bodies!

Place atop all this reconstituted harmony a Sovereign Pontificate of Light, accessible through the Examination of any Church, one that represents the culminating point of all your Science, of all your Faith, of all your Wisdom, and of all your Holiness.

Agarttha will then second your efforts.

But where is this sovereign pontificate? In Rome itself, yes, in Rome, as I have demonstrated earlier.

Take the time to reread all that I said in *Mission of the Sovereigns* and in *Mission of the Jews* about the political role the Papacy has been forced to play up to Pius IX and the most recent Council.[†]

This role has been rendered henceforth impossible, and the evolution of papal duties toward a Sovereign Pontificate of purely intellectual and purely social arbitration is certain to occur, albeit slowly.

You have witnessed up to the present moment popes who were the Roman emperors of their Church, and there was good reason why this was temporary in the long gestation of the current civilization.

But there are social organs similar to the works of a watch, and

---

*[French Revolution. —*Trans.*]
†[The First Vatican Council, 1869–1870. —*Ed.*]

while those that correspond to the minute hand march quickly and in a way that is visible to the eye, the progress of others, although beyond the grasp of the faculty of sight, is nonetheless moving the hand of the hours that are centuries to our collective mind.

Without any higher authority, you emperors and kings of Europe, or presidents of republics, you are condemned to the mutual destruction of your Peoples, your Powers, and your Potencies, as well as to dualism, or rather to a duel between the governed and those who govern of your nations.

This mortal law of anarchy and death, all of whose secret causes I have revealed to you, can no more be abrogated by you than by those revolutionaries who attempt to usurp your thrones and scepters in order to substitute politicians from the bottom in the place of those from the top.

Dualism of any kind can never be abrogated except through the action of Trinitarianism.

This is why it is necessary for an Authority to rise above you that is disarmed of all violent means and which, supported by all the teaching bodies of your continent, abstains from all dogmatic arbitrariness. This Authority is naught but a supreme Arbitrator of your mutual quarrels and internal debates.

And if I advise you to take the Papacy as the culminating point and the axis of this magisterial evolution, it is because if you do not, then instead of a European and Christian Sovereign Pontificate, which you may indeed not want, you will have another ruler within the coming century, but one who is Asiatic and reinforced by a universitarian supervisory board, whose mind will most certainly make the intellectual and social synthesis that you proved yourself unworthy of comprehending and incapable of achieving.

Oh! If Synarchy was simply a personal system, do you believe I would be able to find the inner strength to preach this way?

But it is the very organizational law of every human society, and it is Trinitarian in nature for the very good reason that there is not a single scientific law that is not threefold in nature.

This is the reason why all the scholarly bodies of Antiquity, all issued from Agarttha, all the Epopts, all the social reformers until Moses, Orpheus, and Numa, have always erected Synarchic Law anew or attempted to restore the condition in which it could be achieved.

But here, the Greek Priests or Protestant pastors, the rabbis of the synagogues, the thirty-three-degree Masons, and the professors of our secular universities, reading this work for the first time and unaware of my previous books, will perhaps say: You are taking us back to the clericalism of the Middle Ages.

The exact opposite is true, and this is why, setting aside all personal considerations—since such important matters leave me no room for authorial vanity or literary esteem—I permit myself to urge you to read and reread all my *Missions*.

I have written them for all of you, for your personal salvation, and if I had listened to nothing but my tastes and concern for my personal happiness, never would I have published anything whatsoever.

Whoever may have read my works will not be able, in good conscience, to accuse me of political clericalism, nor of sectarianism of any kind, for my sole concerns are the social sciences and arts, and if I were motivated by any kind of political ambition, I could have satisfied it a long time ago at much less expense and without so much work.

I have said and I repeat that in my Synarchic organization, there is no question of imposing dogmas on anyone, no matter who they are.

Therefore, in the Assembly of a Supreme Council of European Teachings, all a Sovereign Pontiff must do is to respect all that exists, give it his blessing, unite it in the same spirit of tolerance, and gather together all the teaching bodies at last reunited, in one bundle of Light, Wisdom, and Authority.

And I add that European civilization has advanced enough, and that its teaching Faculties have been developed enough, that a universal Sovereign Pontiff could not exist here except at this price.

You do not want it? You would not form part of this Judeo-Christian Synarchy? So be it, that's your business.

But while you are burying yourself deeper within all your intellectual, political, and social anarchies, Asia will be rebuilding itself—have no doubt about that! In accordance with its original Synarchy, and with your two Testaments in hand, it will achieve, without you and even against you if necessary, the universal social promise that they contain.

Why do I say against you if necessary? Because if you do not alter your colonial regime in accordance with Synarchic principles, your African and Asian colonies will inevitably free themselves from your grip; and while, within Europe itself, you become increasingly snarled militarily and economically in the grinding gears of your general government's Anarchy, meanwhile the federation of Asian peoples, including the Arabs, will draw tighter together in a single amphictyonic body around Agarttha.

This holy Agarttha that I am revealing to you in the present book is preeminently antisectarian and far from using its influence over Asia to counter a European Synarchy; it is waiting only for a gesture from you in this direction, before it can give you little by little the fraternal communion of all the sciences and arts that are contained in its secret Mysteries, and whose entire nomenclature our own admirable Judeo-Christian religion holds in its own texts.

Since the time of Ram, do not forget, it is the white race that even in Asia has assumed the seven-crowned tiara and seized the scepter bearing the ram's head, without excluding the other races nevertheless, as testified by the current Brâhatmah, who attained his position by merit alone.

Coming to an understanding is therefore quite easy, just as easy as it is desirable and essential.

With Agarttha, your supreme Synarchic Council will rebuild the universal and cyclical Covenant of all the peoples and all the races of this Earth, and will achieve all the resurrections of nations promised in God's name by the Judeo-Christian prophets.

But without Synarchy, you have nothing at all of the organic European Law that will enable you to achieve this Great Work.

You do not have the neutral and common terrain necessary to come together without confusion.

You do not have the instrument for modifying your colonial regime.

And you, Agartthians, as I have said to those among you whom I have known, it is not a son who is speaking to you in me within this *Mission* and the ones that preceded it, but a brother, whose completely spontaneous initiation owes you nothing except through good will.

It is therefore not Supremacy but Alliance that is involved in the relation we share.

As a Synarchist restoring to Judeo-Christianity your own Spirit of Universality and its own, I have made my testimonies: I am now awaiting yours.

This being said in complete divine and human fraternity, I will now continue my discussion of your institutions and Mysteries, with the same level of respect.

The current Brâhatmah ascended the pontifical throne in 1848, under difficult circumstances over which he was able to prevail thanks to his lofty and wise perspective.

Knowing that God in his designs, while the general government of Anarchy continues to exist, will allow for one evil to be driven out by another, he views the temporary occupation of the provinces of southern India by England as an ordeal imposed from on high.

He knows that this occupation will come to an end when the reasons for it have borne their fruit; he knows the exact hour of the Covenant or of the deliverance.

This is the reason why his moderating authority has always calmed any incautious impatience and been critical of the use of any violent means.

Among the signs that the Deity has caused to pass before his meditations, there is one that is most extraordinary and most secret.

But in order to make it comprehensible to the reader, it is essential that I reveal to him or her yet more of certain Mysteries.

From all points on the globe, whether it is day or night, every initiate of Agarttha sees the spiritual body of this Association as an immense triangle of Light, or, if you prefer, a Pyramid of Fire rising in ethereal Space.

This Yogina is formed from its base to its summit by the spiritual flame of the souls of the Pundits, the Bagwandas, the Archis, the Mahatma, the Mahanga, and finally the Brâhatmah.

This vision is before the eyes of every initiate because this three-cornered Synarchic combination is the very image, in the Ether itself, of the Spiritual Creation and the Trinitarian Order that is maintained by the support and the harmony of all these good wills.

I refer the reader here to what I said in *Mission of the Jews* concerning the Creative Power of Man, either for good, as in the present case, or for evil, as is the case with the violent associations that have been birthed by the Schism of Irshu.

The sign of the Covenant given by the Deity to the spiritual Synarchic body, formed anew by Ram nine thousand years ago, and visible today to all his initiates, is an immense Ring of Cosmic Light with chromatic colors, which envelops the base of the upper third of the Triangle with its closed fluidic arc.

This shows the true extent of the Mysteries of the holy human associations and of the consecration the Deity bestows on those of good will who harmonize within it the hierarchy of their efforts to attain Science and Wisdom.

Since the time of Irshu and the time of Çakya Muni, the closed nature of the Ring of Cosmic Light that envelops the pyramidal symbol of their association has signified, for the high initiates of Agarttha, the fact that divine Providence opposes the Anarchy of the general government of Earth with the Law of the Mysteries. It has also signified the prohibition of allowing the treasures of science into the outside world, where they could only lend Evil an incalculable strength.

In 1877, a date that is of divine memory in my life,* the Brâhatmah saw with his own eyes what is described below. After him, by degrees, the high initiates contemplated the same Sign.

The Cosmic Ring slowly drew away, just as if that of the Planet Saturn were to gape open before the telescopes of our astronomers.

In succession it split up before the eyes of the Sovereign Pontiff, then before those of his assessors, then before those of his Supreme Magic Council.

Suffice it to say that these divisions came to an end when they reached twelve in number, after they had passed through the arithmological and morphological progressions that are the absolute symbols of the Generation of the Primal Principles and the Formation of all Harmony.

After having consulted the celestial intelligences on what meaning to grant these signs, the Supreme College of Agarttha, guided by its own venerable leader, saw in it a direct order from God announcing the gradual abrogation of the law of the Mysteries and the return of Humanity, sufficiently prepared by the living Spirit of Judeo-Christianity, to the Trinitarian Law of its organization.

Is there any need for me to repeat here what I said in *Mission of the Jews*? For Moses, the living Zodiac formed by the twelve Tribes of Israel, the identical image of the ancient Iswara-El, was the symbol of the Harmony of all the peoples in the Trinitarian Law of their universal Covenant.

Is there any need for me to add that in Sanskrit, Iswara-El means and expresses again the idea of God's general government—an intellectual government of Science, Justice, and Economy?

---

*[1877 was the date of Saint-Yves' marriage to Marie Victoire (born de Riznitch)—hence this date being of divine memory to him. —*Ed.*]

I am only unveiling the preceding Mystery to show the Agartthians that I am authorized, not only by the Spirit of Christianity but also by that of the Ramid Cycle from which the ray of the reforms of Abraham and Moses emerged, to reveal (as I did in my previous *Missions* and am doing in this one) all the hidden reserves of the general government of Synarchy, and its antinomy, Nimrodian Anarchy.

As for the surprise that will be caused in all European minds by the Mystery of the Symbol that the Agartthians see everywhere before them, it will give way to contemplation if they only attentively reread their own holy Testaments.

This was also how the Israelites in the Wilderness saw Sinai on fire and could see, from any point in their camp, a column of cloud during the day and a column of flame at night.

It was also in this way that the first initiates of Christ saw him.

In the same manner, under Constantine, the Christian legions, unconscious servants of a political cause, could still nonetheless see in their pure faith the divine *Labarum** illuminating the skies.

Thus finally reunited by Synarchic law, the Judeo-Christians of the Promise, and with them the other human communions, will see standing on the clouds, surrounded by Angels, Spirits, and the Souls of the Saints, the Glorious Body of Christ; and behind the solar halo of his head, the Triangle of Fire bearing the sacred Name of IÊVÊ.

---

*[The *Labarum* is a Roman military standard that was the object of worship by the soldiers. —*Trans.*]

Chapter Three

Man is a reed, the weakest in nature, but as Pascal noted, he is a thinking reed.

As a finishing touch I will add an accent of certitude to the sorrowful whisper of this desperate believer.

Man is a cosmogonic mind, the most powerful in the Universe; he exists as the living reflection of the Deity.

Visible and invisible at the same time, his feet rest on the empire of the demons and at his head is Christ above all the angels, who is the eternal Logos made flesh.

So then, just what is the thought that leads to Science, and what is the Science that leads to Wisdom?

What is the Wisdom girded by the Crown of the Worlds, if not God himself clothed in all his celestial and terrestrial humanity, both visible and invisible to the eyes of flesh?

But these same eyes of flesh, illuminated by Science, purified by Art, sanctified by Faith, can see not only in material clarity but also to its source: the absolute light of spirits and souls.

And then, just what is it they see?

They see the reality of all the sacred Mysteries that all the Faith of all the peoples, around their learned initiators, has always proclaimed and still venerates even today, and will respect all the more once Science and Religion mutually verify one another everywhere.

Yes, millions of souls faithful to this ancient harmony of Science and Religion still see today, as their ancestors saw during the times of the Prophets of Israel and the Hierophants of the entire world, the visions of the All Powerful, the dazzling brilliance of the Veil that covers the heavenly Tabernacle of the God of Total Knowledge.

Yes, everything that the Prophets of all your Sanctuaries have told you, everything their voices are still singing through the sacred harmonies of your cathedrals, churches, and temples, in the breath of the choirs and in the winds of the holy organs—yes, all of this is the Truth.

And this universal harmony incessantly makes known among you the ineffable majesty of God, his worshipful providence, and his inexpressible bounty, only while speaking to you at the same time of the celestial grandeur of Man and the Perfection of the divine purpose toward which his Perfectibility returns.

This purpose is the glorification of God in Man and of Man in God; and this divine term, toward which universal Religion through all its denominations and cults is leading you, is identical to the term that Science, on its highest peaks of enlightenment, delivered unto itself, will eventually finally see again, by verifying Faith.

The same apogee of civilization is spontaneously glimpsed, not only by the learned but by all poets worthy of the name. It is these poets who, keeping intact the purity of their sacred powers of intuition, are the watchmen of the night and the lookouts for our nations.

All the great historians verify a posteriori what the direct sight of the seers perceives in the future, and all well-informed sociologists and economists do naught but repeat, in other styles, what the Science of Antiquity shouted to the four winds through all its holy voices and all its prophetic or Sibylline colleges, from the time of

Zoroaster to that of David, from the time of Isaiah to that of the Voluspa.*

And what, in short, is this purpose of Humanity?

It is a purpose that is as practical as it is grandiose, and because it is simple, it is divinely and humanly true.

Like every individual—invisible or visible—every collective being has its law, and this law is Trinitarian for the reason that every law is the expression of a relationship between two terms.

Those who govern or who are governed in Europe, those who are conquerors or conquered in Asia, you all have an equal vested interest in the return of Humanity to this social law of the Kingdom of God, which is nothing other than his right, within which your own rights are encompassed.

No, egotism is not at all true, whether it be that of an individual or a people, a race or an entire Continent.

France experienced this in 1789; its most noble thinkers grasped this truth, but sectarian and violent politicians bankrupted the nation's good will, which had specifically illuminated the feeling of Universality.

Liberty, Equality, Fraternity: this great Ramid, Abramite, and Christian phrase, expressed in *Telemachus* by Fénelon, would have been as erudite and religious as it was social, if only greater pains had been taken to understand and develop it rather than distort it by exploiting it politically.

There can only be freedom in unbounded Space, and the limitless space of the human mind is nothing other than the Mind of God.

There can only be equality in one same law of harmony, and this law of harmony embraces the constitution of the entire social body.

There is no fraternity possible unless freedom and equality are understood in this way.

But all of this is precisely the opposite of the mutual Anarchy of political governments and the egotistical brutality that presides not only

---

*[The Voluspa, which means the Prophecy of the Wise Woman or Seeress, is the first part of the Poetic Edda. It is a story of creation addressed to Odin. —*Trans.*]

over the relations of Christian peoples with each other, but over the relations of their Colonial regime toward other continents and other communities of believers.

In vain will the English declare: "No matter. We took it and we shall keep it."

I hear in Isaiah and in Ezekiel the fall of the emporocratic government of Tyre.

The fate of the Phoenicians awaits the English if they do not alter their colonial rule using Synarchic means.

In vain will the Prussians say: "We conquered it and we are keeping it."

I hear the response of Daniel, Sovereign Pontiff not only of the Jews but of the Chaldeans; I hear his prophecies concerning all the violent empires.

These predictions are not the fruits of a delirious imagination, but are the products of an exact science, one that is as precise as our own mathematics.

Close to eighty centuries of experiments have already validated them, and every empire that has ruled by the sword has perished by the sword.

In vain will the Russians say: "Let us go and overturn the colonial empire of England."

Though they will be welcomed as liberators, sooner or later they will be expelled as conquerors unless, in accordance with Synarchic Law, they bring about social redemption at the same time as political liberation.

But how much blood and gold, how much weeping and mourning, how much desolation and devastation will we be spared if, thanks to this Law, they become one with England and with Europe and all together aid the people of Asia to form with us the great and holy Alliance that is at the heart of all their memories, all their Science, and all their Faith, just as it is for ours!

A chimera, the skeptics will cry! Are they then taking politics for a reality, until the time when historical experiences shall cease to be a lesson for them?

Can anything then follow other than lunacy and an infernal nightmare—this system of violence given new life by Nimrod of Babylon, this armed Anarchy of the general government of Europe, its ruinous footing for war, the suffering and instability of all our nations, the impotence of the Judeo-Christian religions subject to these politics, and finally the dull rumblings or explosive thunderclaps of the revolutions sown everywhere by these causes of death?

A house constructed in this way is not truly built, but must be erected anew with the same materials, while respecting each of them but grouping them on more solid foundations that conform better to our needs, in such a way that the entire edifice, fulfilling the eternal laws of the social sciences and arts, may take on the complete shape that is appropriate to our simultaneously scientific and Christian civilization.

Are you going to wait for the revolutionaries to do this for you?

Throughout all of history the revolutionaries have demolished things; in none of these instances have they been seen rebuilding.

As a consequence of the anarchy of all governments over the last five thousand years, the revolution of those who are governed cannot be halted unless the former repeals its own status by achieving Synarchy.

Then, everything that is legitimate in the revolutionary protest of the multitudes will change into their consent to an Authority that is clearly distinguished from a Power. This will be an international renewed and authorized Authority, and finally an economic power that will restore solidarity among the interests of all classes.

Here, I shall allow myself to address my words to the crowned son of the most noble of martyrs.

Sire!
The immense edifice constructed by Your fathers is not only the living shield of Europe against any military attempt from Asia, it is

the vanguard of Judeo-Christianity and the whole of Christianity, even in Asia.

The purpose of the Christian Promise is identical in all its social scope to the ancient spirit of science and wisdom, whose Tradition has been piously kept in the Temple that is the subject of this book.

This Temple reveres Moses and Jesus Christ as much as we do, and all the Mysteries of the Hebrew text of our divine Testaments are scientifically known and proven there.

If the poor organization of the general government and the colonial regime of Europe dictates that, sooner or later, Your armies should collide in Asia against those of England, then in the name of God, profit from everything I have revealed to You in this book.

Sire, have caution when touching Afghanistan and do not advance into the territory of these amphictyons without pronouncing the ancient password of the Kingdom of God.

Like Philip of Macedonia in Delphi and like Alexander in Asia, may Your Majesty make the Synarchic rallying sign at the Temple of which I speak; this will prevent the initiates from confusing You with the oppressive and sectarian conquerors.

Then, if, in the regions of India, England does not bring about its downfall by establishing Synarchy, Providence will put wind in your sails, because marching in the footsteps of Ram, Sire, You will only have fought in the name of the Christ and Saint Michael, the Solar Archangel, to redeem the peoples after having freed them.

The peoples of Central Asia feel great sympathy toward Russia and toward its sovereign.

Karelian Celts in the north and west, Turanian Celts or Scythians in the south, the Russian people have atavistic affinities with all the divisions of the white race, not only in Europe but also in Asia.

We even can find traces in these Caucasian populations of the ancient black race, amalgamated with the white, and some princes make no secret of a genealogy going back to the Abramites and even to the Celtic Bodhons.*

I have indicated elsewhere, based on local memories, the remnants of the ancient Ramid Empire both in legends and in the stone monuments of the tiered valleys of the great mountain [*sic*] that separates Europe from Asia.

These memories exist below the earth's surface as well as above it, and more than once, even in this century, certain initiates have descended underground to visit the stone libraries, and have not returned empty-handed.

The deeply religious sentiment of the Russian masses, their instinctive occultism, their language, their legends, their prophecies, and the Hermetic interpretation that some sects keep of the sacred scriptures, are all so many ties indicative of an intellectual and social alliance with Asia.

Far be it from me to think of comparing the Russians to the English here!

Although my works might enlighten politicians on many things of which they know nothing, they are not the works of a political man.

But it is impossible to conceal the fact that the Russians will be inevitably compelled to become terrible auxiliary forces for the liberation of Asia if England, for want of intelligence, wisdom, and humanity, does not take the measures necessary to prevent and satisfy the explosion of independence that the end of this century will certainly witness.

It could easily do so by generously providing the Hindus with more reforms than this people perhaps might grant themselves once they were freed.

Now this would be a surer path for England to take than allying with Germany to set China loose on Russia.

---

*[A nomadic tribe of Celts, remote ancestors of the Hebrew people according to Fabre d'Olivet. —*Trans.*]

Here, I would like to permit myself to address my words to a queen.*

Madam,

Your Majesty, may you deign to pardon the liberty I am taking, for which love of humanity is the sole excuse and sole motive.

A loyal intellectual understanding with the university Temple of Agarttha is the sole measure that can maintain beneath Your scepter the immense populations of Your colonial Indian Empire.

Your Majesty is capable of fulfilling a much more considerable role than ever before, which would be that of a supreme arbitrator who is equally learned and wise.

At the head of a European nation that is one of the torchbearers of our civilization, everything would be easy for You, following the luminous and pacific paths that Humanity commands me to point out here.

Dare, Madam, to craft an understanding between Your government and that of Russia.

Dare, Madam, with the emperor of this great country, to summon as witness of Your peaceful efforts the whole of European civilization, and together ask the Temple of Agarttha to open itself loyally to You, while you guarantee its independence.

You will have rendered Europe an incalculable service and, in accord with this Temple and the Tsar, the three of you serving as representatives of all the science and faith that our two continents hold, You will have surely preserved for England the civic rights that, in India, will be much more solid than the right of conquest that forms the basis of Your current empire in this country.

There are already three orders of Liberty, Equality, and Fraternity that the old Indian civilization has requested, and here they are.

They have requested mixed universities, they have requested

---

*[The author is addressing Queen Victoria. —*Trans.*]

mixed tribunals, and finally they have requested economic arbitration to reduce the crushing burdens their populations have been forced to bear.

I know that Your Majesty's enlightened government has itself desired to see this kind of understanding established, but that the interests of the European colonists there have been, to a certain extent, opposed.

However, it is there that salvation lies today, and it is there that Your subjects will find the Synarchic foundations for the civic rights of tomorrow.

India has no wish to rise up in revolt: its better-inspired ancient wisdom asks for naught but its own life and its own resurrection.

More fortunate than Semiramis who tried in vain to conquer it, Your Majesty can, in the name of the whole of Christianity, help it to reconstruct itself and to draw from an intellectual and social alliance with Your great Celtic people the powerful and propitious energies necessary for the union of this center of civilization and our own.

Furthermore, a Synarchic understanding with Europe would hardly be an innovation; it would be nothing other than the realization of the plan for European and colonial reforms on which England and France have collaborated together on other occasions.

Queen Elizabeth [the First] found agreement with Henri IV [of France] and with Sully on this project for a Social Constitution that would have ensured World Peace, and avoided so many revolutions and wars.

Thanks to the ancient Celtic-Scandinavian institutions of the English, their colonial regime is greatly superior to those of all the other European peoples, with the exception of Holland.

But for lack of a Synarchic constitution, open through examination to all individuals of all races, their establishment in India possesses radical vices, the least of which is foreign domination and a failure to bring, thus far, any added intellectual or social value in exchange for the material exploitation that hobbles this eldest of all civilizations.

I am perfectly well aware that English domination is at least on a par with that of the various conquerors who followed each other in succession in India, but it does not constitute an alliance, and this last condition is essential for the reform and preservation of this colony.

If the double authority of universal History and the holy books is worth anything in such matters, one will find their teachings faithfully examined and summarized in my two previous books: *Mission of the Sovereigns* and *Mission of the Jews*.

In the first, going to the root of the causes of the anarchy of the general European government, I provided a sufficiently complete ethical portrait of diplomacy in chapters IX, X, and XI to have no need to revisit the matter here.

I challenge political men worthy of this name to study and pay attention to what I call the Anglo-Russian Binome and its direct opposition in Central Asia.

The question of Herat and Afghanistan should be given particular emphasis.

I will now permit myself to address a few words to those initiates of Agarttha who would like to read these works and form a well-founded opinion of them.

No sectarian motive is prompting my efforts, no political interest is guiding my pen, and no personal consideration has impelled or hindered me in the completion of the intellectual task I have undertaken, a work whose crown is the present book.

If I address, as I have just done, the Russian and English sovereigns and peoples, if I have urged them toward an understanding with Agarttha after having demonstrated its vital importance, then let me say once more that it is solely my responsibility, and is due to my initiative alone.

I believe this understanding is as essential for the renaissance of India as it is for the crowning achievement of European civilization.

It is my sincere wish, following the designs of God that are written in the Vedas as well as in the Hebrew text of our [Old and New] Testaments, and in [the Arabic of] the Koran itself, that the universal Alliance of the days of Antiquity should soon be restored.

The twentieth century of the Christian Era will see its fulfillment upon the foundations whose principles I have examined through the events of history and in the depths of our holy books.

Now, to speak of Alliance is not to speak of merging, but of harmony between all the differences of the various parts.

Your Venerable University piously preserves all of the past, all of its memory, all of its sciences, and all of its arts.

Our own universities, including the synagogues and all the churches, are no less deserving of their place, and their sympathies toward you are no less necessary than an opening to your Mysteries is essential to us.

It is through this fraternal understanding that all the faculties of the human mind can lend themselves mutual assistance, realizing anew the Promise made by our religious founders and by yours.

In vain will a few ill-wishers in Europe say that I am trying to turn Christianity into Brahmanism; in vain will a few fools repeat this by hearsay.

In vain will the same calumny in reverse be brought against me in Asia, claiming that I seek to reduce Brahmanism and Buddhism to the dogmatism of our various churches.

My works defend themselves against such imputations, as well as against many others.

Agarttha forms what Moses called the Council of the Earlier Cycles, and what Saint Paul called the Church of the Protogonos. This should be sufficient to make every believer respect it as a Religion, and every scholar respect it as a university.

Moses himself urged his initiates to listen to the teachings of this Council, and Jethro was one of the pontiffs who remained faithful to its scientific Tradition.

Finally, even in the Hebrew text of the New Testament, we find the name of Agarttha at the head of each of the epistles, not to mention a good many other passages. Here the veil of the Covenant of the Ancient Iswara-el with Mosaic Israel is lifted no more than is appropriate; likewise the first Christian initiation with the university temple of Paradesa.

The irrefutable demonstrations of all these truths have already been made, and will be shown to the light of day at their rightful time by the individual who has the right to do so. This will take place in various countries, as I have said on many occasions, but only at such time when the first Chamber of Synarchy will have been created.

Then we will know what a true scientific exegesis of the sacred texts consists of; and then, as it is said in the Scriptures, the Law, in other words the Science of divine and human things, will be verified unto the Iod.

For the moment, it is from another point of view that I address my words to the members of the Supreme Council of Agarttha.

The sacred sign that manifested before you in 1877 summoned you, among other things, to guarantee your sovereignty as an independent territorial power.

Russia is already brushing the head of your confederation in Afghanistan.

The armed violence employed by England in Burma is already almost touching the foot of your amphictyonic body.

This is why the Mystery, which has allowed you to preserve your Synarchy up to now, can cause you to lose it—if you maintain it.

In fact, the whole of Christendom knows nothing of you, and the immense moral support that can be lent you by its Governments, its Universities, its Religions, the Unknown Superiors of its Freemasonry, and finally its Public Opinion, is all something that you lack at this time, and it is essential for your independence, if you wish to keep it.

What would happen if I had not taken the initiative of revealing your Synarchy, your Wisdom, and the importance of your University? Here is what would happen:

In the space of a few short years, without Europe even suspecting your existence, you would be caught and blockaded, as Jerusalem once was, in the mutual embrace of four military empires: emporocratic England, Russia, the Islam of the Turkomans, and finally China, still governed at the present hour by Turanian Tartars.

Christendom, without suspecting the catastrophes unconsciously prompted by its diplomatic constitution, without suspecting what it was losing by your downfall accompanied and followed by horrendous cataclysms, would hear from the Far East naught but the sound of armies, the roar of cannon, and would see naught on the slopes of the Himalayas but a plume of smoke shot through by flames, a prelude to the conflagration of all of Asia.

This is why, authorized by the living spirit of Christ, the Abramites, and the Ramids, I have opened the Manavic veil that covers you, and this is the reason why I am saying to you: Come out of the Invisible, show yourself little by little to all of Synarchic Europe with open hands and arms, with all your credentials of past glory, present utility, and future benevolence.

Tell all of our Teaching Institutions just what you have in store for them.

For the synagogues and the churches, the keys to the Kabbalistic interpretation of the Hebrew texts of the Old and New Testament, the keys to all the miracles they relate, the keys to all the sciences and all the arts one can sense between the lines therein, will be like the marching pilgrim's steps that awaken a dull rumbling in underground passageways in certain sacred, solitary places.

Tell our skeptics what you say among yourselves, that Judeo-Christianity is true, that the Christ is the preeminent Messiah, and that his glorious second coming will be accomplished through the reconstitution of a worldwide social State in his eternal Law.

To our scientists, from the chemists and physicists to the physiologists, from the naturalists to the archaeologists, from the psychologists to the astronomers, say: "We are bringing to you five hundred and fifty-six centuries of memories, observations, and experiments that span a space from the center of the globe to the summit of the heavens."

Finally, to the chapters of the thirty-third degrees of Freemasonry, say: "All that you have promised we are able to keep, and this promise we will keep for those who, within our Temple, fulfill the conditions required by the Examination."

Then, enveloped as by a new cosmic ring by Judeo-Christian public opinion, place yourselves under the protection of its Religions, its Universities, its Governments, and its Masonic Temples; and like all the other independent powers of Asia, protect yourselves with our Public Law, for what little it may still be worth.

It is sufficient that this law might be perfectible, and that the suggestion of Synarchic ideas that I have renovated in human understanding might continue to spread there, events responding to it.

These events, the fruits of an Anarchy that has endured for close to five thousand years, will not fail to provide increasing verification of the necessity for Synarchy.

Believe me, my brothers in Christ, therein lies your social salvation, just as much as ours.

Consult within your sealed sanctuaries the Eternal One, His Angels, His Powers, the souls of your Pontiffs and Saints: their response cannot be doubted.

Protected by our common law, you will no longer have to fear that the secret actions of any State or Sect may threaten either your social existence or your intellectual life.

You will not have any need to dread the abstraction, destruction, or alteration of your texts, which are impossible to understand if you do not personally deliver the Dorian key and indicate the secrets of the lock.

Our various teaching establishments, by supervising each other, will prevent the predominance of any form of sectarianism in the examination that you will generously invite the whole of Christianity to undergo.

Finally, in order to pass from the public law of today to the

Synarchic Covenant of tomorrow, it will be sufficient that among us circumstances allow for a Sovereign Pontiff to rise to the head of the entire Judeo-Christian social body; to restore its Authority and synthetic spirit; and—supported by the consciousness of all peoples who are heedful of the intonations of Truth—to call upon all governments to submit to the Law of intelligence and love that must recombine and reorganize them.

It is then that with your support, the same Law will reunite all Asiatic and African peoples with each other, as well as with us.

It is then that all the rebirths of which I have spoken shall be achieved, from the banks of the Nile to the banks of the Tigris and the Euphrates, from Baghdad to Jerusalem.

It is then that, finally, with the neutralization of all the Holy Cities, the renewal of Earth itself will take place as predicted by the prophets.

And the deserts once inhabited by men and covered by cities will grow green again. Once more they will be filled with gushing springs, rivers, peoples, and metropolises.

Ah! I am well aware, however, that the cyclical return of Humanity to this Kingdom of God will not be achieved effortlessly.

Armed to the teeth by Western technology, the Evil inaugurated by Irshu will not abdicate easily.

There will be yet more martyred peoples, and the general government of trickery and violence will continue for some time to eclipse the government that Moses called the very reflection of God.

The Antigod and the Antichrist designated by Daniel will continue to caress the apocalyptic Beast, the brutality that presides over relations between nations, social states, and continents.

Even the believers will still tell themselves, despite the Abramites, despite Moses, despite Our Lord Jesus Christ: "Let us arm ourselves," because the bloody law of the Babylonian Bull will forever prevent the radiant face of the God of Complete Knowledge from again appearing by means of the reopening of the Universal Alliance of Antiquity.

But may all the world's politicians know this full well: the believers, to whom initiation has given Certitude following Faith, are less naïve than the governmental skeptics and materialists.

They watch Evil opposing itself, weakening itself as it becomes more generalized, and they wait.

I have shown in *Mission of the Sovereigns* and *Mission of the Jews,* by unmasking all the causes of all the various forms of Anarchy, how far from naïve this Spirit of Science and Love that presides over Synarchy actually is.

I have left in safe hands a testament of the universal reorganization of this latter entity.

May the believers be reassured: I am not opposing politics to itself here, but only contrasting Science with Ignorance and Wisdom with Folly.

I was going to show to their eyes the enumeration of the peoples of Aries and the Lamb, and of those who still bear the mark of the schism of the Bull.

I was going to cause them to count these people in Europe, in Asia, and in the other parts of the world, and evaluate their intellectual and physical strengths, and what their past, summarized in the present, promises for their future.

I was going to add to this scene all the necessary alliances of the Aryan peoples with each other, from continent to continent, and their certain chances of saving themselves and of recovering the leadership of that civilization whose initiators they were.

But the more my penetration of divine wisdom gave me a clear view into the secrets of the intergovernmental Anarchy of Earth, the less able I was to demean the flag of Ram, of the Abramites, and of Jesus, and to let it fall into the dark and bloody spheres of collective passions.

No, with my eyes fixed on the Heavenly City and the Glorious Christ, I could now only see all humanity as the separated members of one and the same divine body.

Ever since the sacrifice made on Calvary, there have no longer been any Turanians, and the general government of men by force, decapitated of its Babylonian apotheosis by the Christ, will not be able to prevail any longer against the Return of the Kingdom of God.

Human consciousness and intelligence are too free today from the spirit of race, lineage, and sect for there to be need for any weapons other than Science in the Redemption not only of individuals but of the entire terrestrial Social State.

And this consciousness, and this intelligence, illuminated by all the concentric rays of Science and Faith, are no longer the monopoly of any one people or any one race.

In this integral Catholicism, the Turanians and Aryans no longer appear to me as anything more than Souls, just as they would appear beneath the subterranean dome where your sages celebrate their Mysteries, and where the chromatic colors make it impossible to distinguish any difference of skin, or any difference of features.

All men are good, and they do evil only because they believe their self-interest demands it.

All of them wish for good, each in his own manner; but they do not know how to reconcile their many wishes and the many things they desire.

There is a social Law of Harmony that will make this holy reconciliation, this Divine Union, possible among all individuals and among all societies.

Under a thousand names, taking a thousand shapes, through a thousand different languages, for five thousand years we have been doing our utmost to maintain, in every direction and in all nations, the memory and hope of this law, which is the Trinitarian symbol of our Alliance in God.

This law was made flesh from the bosom of God to the womb of a woman; it is called Jesus, it is named Jesus Christ.

It is He that I worship in this law, it is this law that I worship in Him, and although I attribute to the authority [of Him and this law] all the intellectual and moral strengths that they increase a hundred-fold in me, I feel myself, before them as before Divine Humanity, to be nothing but a small flame held in a pinch of dust.

And this cyclical Authority, which speaks so strongly through me, only makes me understand all the more powerfully both my own humility and my own powerlessness to proclaim Synarchy appropriately and serve it as it deserves.

This is the reason I am shouting to the four winds, invoking everywhere the souls and sacred reserves promised for our fidelity.

It is they who will carry out what I wish I could achieve, if this be the work of the entire human mind in accord with the divine mind—supplied with all the leverage that I am lacking.

And now, may I be permitted to raise my voice humbly toward the venerated leader of my Religion.

Most Holy Father,

It is by design that in this book I have permitted myself to piously touch upon, by invoking them, the pontifical summits of Humanity.

In the prophecies of our holy Church, Pius IX called himself the cross of crosses, the decrucified cross.

Your sovereign pontificate, Most Holy Father, heralds a light in the sky, *Lumen in Cælo*.

This light, in fact, illuminates the sacred path of future sovereign pontiffs.

Soon, realizing what was once predicted by the inspired of Ireland, they will be able to glorify Christ by preaching the peace of the Human race to the nations: *Gloria olivæ,* the glory of peace, and hence the radiance of Wisdom and Science.

For this reason, I take the religious and filial liberty of raising up toward Your Holiness my four *Missions*.

During this difficult time of twilight preceding the new age, I do not ask Your Holiness for either a public judgment or a blessing for these works, but simply that they be studied by the scholars, sages, and saints subject to Your Venerable Discipline and enlightened by Your erudite and prudent impetus.

A faithful layman of the Spirit of Moses and Christianity, I have undoubtedly said nothing in my works that is not already known by the most studious of these respectable guardians of Catholic Universality and the entire divine Tradition.

As Fénelon advised, I have pushed my intelligence and faith to their limits to follow the path trodden before me by the Fathers of the Universal Church, from the time of the Alexandrians up to Gerson.*

I have had no fear of putting my Catholic mentality and Christian faith to the test of the Universality of the human mind and all the manifestations carried out by the divine Spirit in the Science and wisdom of all times and all peoples.

It is not my prerogative to say whether, as a Catholic and a Christian, I have emerged from this formidable ordeal victorious.

It is up to the priests of all our religions and the scholars of all our universities to examine what I have done.

This is why, addressing myself to the summit of this cathedral of intelligences, I dare to ask Your Holiness that a study of my works be carried out under the aegis of His wisdom and of His luminous charity.

I have believed, and still believe, that the time has come, as it did in the time of the Magi, for a great terrestrial renewal, which will be nothing less than the social harvest of what the Apostolic and Militant Church, under the guidance of its Divine Founder, has sowed over the last nineteen centuries in the individual souls.

I have believed, and still believe, that the present time is the dawn of the Second Coming of Our Lord Jesus Christ, the beginning of his learned Glorification through all the limbs of his entire Social body here below.

---

*[Jean de Chalier de Gerson (1363–1429), mystical theologian. —*Trans.*]

I have believed, and still believe, not only in the letter but also in the spirit of the sacred texts, the Mysteries, Sacraments, and Symbols.

As a layman, I have not consulted any priest of any religion, for fear of compelling his disciplinary responsibility against the freedom that the current liberation of these teachings has invited me to take.

But the true meaning of my work would be distorted if it were interpreted as any kind of novation.

This is the reason why, Most Holy Father, I prostrate myself before the feet of Your Holiness as the most humble and respectful of the faithful.

I will not conceal the fact that the preceding letter may perhaps disconcert those minds, in the different Churches and the various regions of the university and philosophical institutions, who have followed the publication of my *Missions* with interest.

As a consequence of all the political confusions that I noted in the history of the General Government of Christianity, the papacy is detested by the Greek Orthodox Church, by the Anglican Church, by the various Protestant Churches, by Freemasonry, and by all the rationalist schools engendered by our secular universities.

We must not conceal this truth or seek to remedy by political means a situation that has been created by politics.

This vicious circle dates from very long ago, and has been sanctioned in European common law by the Republican diplomatic constitution that the leaders of the European nations imposed upon themselves at the Congress of Westphalia in 1648.

I have taken the governmental ethic and esthetic of both Christianity and the Cycle of Ram far enough that I can in no way be suspected of sectarianism.

For this reason, I have no fear of exposing before all the enemies of the papacy the following considerations, confident as I am that they are of a nature to rally them gradually to the principles of social Science and Art, germane to this matter.

The Sovereign Pontificate, which is the culminating point of the European Social State, has been enclosed in the Roman Episcopacy, the Italian Primacy, the Latin Patriarchate, and the Imperialate of the clerics of the Western Church, in much the same way as a principle is occultly concealed within the quadruple envelope of a seed.

The Sovereign Pontificate is this principle; all the rest constitutes nothing but the elements of the seed that must cover it, enable it to take root, and then die there, to be resurrected later, free of all cumbersome complexity.

With the Pontificate of Pius IX [1846–1878], the ancient papacy definitively died, giving up the political life and feudal turmoil of the Middle Ages.

With Leo XIII,* the nonpolitical conditions that allowed for the Sovereign Pontificate ushered in its possible rebirth.

Now, if the Papacy were necessarily both politically ethnic and Roman, might this also be the case for the Sovereign Pontificate, if it wished and needed to be realized intellectually and socially?

The theocratic essence of the Sovereign Pontificate is the synthetic and arbitral Universality of the teachings, the integral Catholicism of a religion, whatever that religion may be.

The Judeo-Christian religion is but one religion in a profound gnosis, just as Judeo-Christianity is but one single body in its divine principle and in its social finality.

The truth of this is so pronounced, not only in the Knowledge but even in the historical proof (in other words, in the coercion exercised by the facts upon the unconscious instincts of our denominations), that the last council† of our Latin Church abdicated of its own accord, feeling itself to be powerless to realize or renew the Catholic doctrine or the standing of Catholicism within contemporary Christianity.

Infallibility, in fact, is nothing other than absolute discretionary

---

*[Leo XIII was Pope from 1878 to 1903; Saint-Yves was writing this in 1886. —*Ed.*]
†[The First Vatican Council, 1869–1870. —*Ed.*]

power, given by the Latin bishops to the Roman Papacy in order to free the Sovereign Pontiff from all sectarianism, so that he might also free these bishops from their own social impotence, along with him and in accordance with the inspiration he would receive from the whole of Christendom and from God.

Here, I address all the Judeo-Christians who do not belong to the Roman communion, permitting myself to tell them to pay very close attention to the facts I just outlined.

Here are some of its possible consequences.

The Sovereign Pontiff who, under the conditions established for him by the most recent Latin council, may wish to obtain full discretionary power and full authority, ex cathedra, in order to achieve the Synarchic reorganization of Europe, for the first time has both the power and the possibility of doing so. This Pontiff is Pius IX.

He can in fact declare that during his lifetime, starting at any given date, every Episcopal nomination and coronation must have the Examination as an absolute precondition.

He can require that this examination be open to all Judeo-Christians without any distinction, either of religion or of priest or lay position, as in the case of Saint Ambrose of Milan and many others, to wit, the entire body of Higher Educators in all our European Universities.

Finally, he can make the sovereign decision that starting with the episcopacy, this precondition of an examination must be maintained and extended up to the post of the Sovereign Pontiff himself, but that now it should be beneath the seal of Initiation.

He will therefore be in a position to determine his successor without excluding any for reasons of sect or race.

Thus, for the first time since the division and diarchy of the Churches of the East and West, the intellectual and social Union of Judeo-Christianity will be realizable.

For the first time since then, it will be possible to effectuate the arbitral Synthesis of the teachings within a supreme Synarchic Council, in complete freedom.

For the first time, the European States, under the guarantee of this great intellectual and arbitral authority, itself supported by the public conscience of Europe, will be able to proceed without danger in the establishment of a general government of Justice, not a government of diplomatic trickery and military antagonism.

For the first time, finally, under the double guarantee of these two Supreme councils, this Teaching Authority and this Power of Justice, it will be possible for emperors, kings, and presidents of republics, forming an integral part of this Power of Justice, to summon the Judeo-Christian nations to the formation of a great economic Assembly.

In this way, Synarchy can be achieved ex cathedra, under the aegis of the European Sovereign Pontiff, and become accessible again to all Judeo-Christians, without excluding any religions, universities, or peoples.

This supranational reorganization is the potential key to the vault of the entire European Social State.

It was this cornerstone that was rejected, as it says in the Gospels, at the moment when the Synarchy of Moses gave way to the political monarchy in Judea.

Among its advantages, it offers the specific feature of not affecting the primacy of ethnic churches anywhere, nor the current position of religions in each nation. Finally, it leaves intact the disciplinary constitutions and primary teachings of each of these religions.

Thus, from deep within the ethnic bias in which the political and feudal conditions of the papacy are perishing, the Sovereign Pontiff can and must surge forth for the benefit of the Universal Church (which is to say the whole Social State), and rebuild the culminating point of the teaching authority.

The peak of the universal, social cathedral, its scientific transfiguration, will no longer appear only as *Urbi,* for today there are as many

*Urbes** as there are capitals, and European civilization no longer has a monopoly on any of them.

It is *Orbi*†—in other words the whole of Universality itself—to which the spirit and reality of this arbitral and culminating function known as the Sovereign Pontiff must correspond.

But, the less thoughtful of my fellow Roman Catholics will say, this would be the end of the Roman Church!

Why?

Nothing will have changed within this Church; the Sovereign Pontiff will continue to be its Patriarch, its specific hierarchy and teachings will remain intact, and all it will have done is to realize its own Catholic agenda—Catholic meaning antisectarian, antipolitical, and universalist.

No longer able nor even wishing to dominate the other communions politically, it will win them back socially by respecting them, and thus accepting them into a truly ecumenical covenant, for the first time since the Greco-Latin diarchy.

Does the current situation of Europe provide indications of such a solution, such a salvaging of all the Churches and all the universities, as well as all the Nation-States?

It appears difficult for me to doubt that this is the case, unless I blind myself completely.

"But Rome," people will say; "what of the entire organization of the Vatican?"

I do not see in what way a Universal Sovereign Pontiff could prove harmful to them, nor what more worthy throne this Vicar of Christ could desire, if it were left to him.

At the current time in Europe, it is impossible to improvise a ceremonial tradition of this supreme importance.

---

*[Latin: cities. —*Ed.*]

†[Latin: orb, sphere, universe. —*Ed.*]

The only possible course is to array oneself in it, in order to bring it into accord with the current and future world, by achieving it in accordance with Synarchic principles.

"But Italy?" people will ask again.

It has no more to lose than the Papacy and the Latin Church, nor more than all the other Communions, nor all the other nations—quite the contrary.

By the mere admission that it no longer wishes to provide a haven for the Sovereign Pontiff, Rome will always be the center of the Latin Patriarchy and the Italian Primacy.

"But Rome is not a free city" will be people's final objection. A free city is required for a Sovereign Pontiff.

To this I respond: for what reason couldn't all the capitals of the civilized world be one day consecrated as free cities by a European Sovereign Pontiff?

This would be a much better solution than having them bombed, in scorn of Christ and of Christianity.

But what about in the meantime?

In the meantime, the Papacy that you find the captive of a political state is no longer what it once was, and one must wisely and scientifically contemplate what it might be in the future.

"Rome is no longer Rome," you will say; "it is the captivity of Avignon."

This would then be the case, as a logical consequence of the general government inaugurated in 1648.

"But," some will ask, "what if the revolution from below, fruit of the revolution from above started in 1648 by the sovereigns themselves, drives the Papacy out of Rome and Italy?"

Then the Pontiff, making his way through Constantinople, clad in white like the clouds, will return to the sacred mountains from whence his office is descended.

Jerusalem! Jerusalem! I hear all the holy prophecies that have predicted your rebirth!

It is from Christ's tomb that the cyclical Synarchy and its Sovereign Pontificate will then be resurrected.

It is here that this Sovereign Pontificate will find its free city, its duties, and its definitive mission.

Yes, its mission, for there is but one European Sovereign Pontificate that, with its seat in this city, will be able to realize the Synarchic Law of the Kingdom of God over the entire Earth, the cyclical Covenant and Peace of all the religions, all the races, and all the continents, in Ramid, Abramite, and Christian Israel.

And if someone tells me that the conversion of the papacy into an ecumenical and universal Sovereign Pontificate, whether it sits in Rome, Constantinople, or Jerusalem, is a novation, I will again respond: No, a thousand times no, the only novation would be if this did not come to pass.

During the lifetime of Jesus, the Judeo-Christian Church and Abramite and Mosaic Israel had only one head—that of Christ—around which shone the halo of Divine Authority that is beyond any and all manner of political compromise.

The Caesarean Church of Constantine, the dismembered Christianity of the crucifixion, was able, thanks to politics, to erect altars against altars, oppose heads against heads, limbs against limbs, cross against cross.

It will be utterly different in the Church of the Glorification and of the General Government of God.

Synarchic in its social body, One in its summit that emerges luminous from the Examination, it will gather together all that politics has divided.

No, there is no question of novation for this formal Promise from the Old and New Testaments: one sole flock, one sole shepherd.

What I have just placed before the eyes of my readers are not my personal ideas but the very perspectives that our own Holy Scriptures have revealed before our time, verified by historical fact.

Let these Mosaic and Christian perspectives of European history and the earlier cycles be removed or suppressed, if you like.

But let us admit that it is the blindness of men of state and men of the cloth, and the mutual hatred of sects and international or national parties, that prevents the advent of this Synarchic Sovereign Pontificate and the reformation of all the Teaching authorities, this Council of Justice of the European States and this Ecumenical council of all the Judeo-Christian nations.

Let us admit the fact that the current stupor and impotence will continue, and that this kind of reawakening of the Faith, Science, intelligence, and entire good sense of our continent is only an impossibility and a chimera.

Let us say that contemporary Europe is the best of all possible worlds; that all its different anarchies are the supreme triumph of Science and Modern Civilization; and that the Synarchic abrogation I recommend, the Sacred Texts, and the History in our hands are not even worth the trouble of being contemplated or given a moment's notice.

But if this is the case, we must then face up to the perspectives that remain open for Europe's future if we eliminate all those mentioned above.

Let us therefore close the Temple of the Kingdom of God and remain outside it, prey to all the dire events unleashed by all these anarchies.

Tiaras, Miters, Crowns, Governments, Nationalities, Universities after Churches, Christendom after Christianity, will all ceaselessly continue to be fodder for destruction, torn between the anarchists on top and the anarchists on the bottom.

Headed by its bishops clad in black habits or military uniforms, official Europe, at odds with itself, will continue gaily leading the funeral procession of our Social State and its civilization, drums beating and cannons primed.

But during this time, kindly cast a glance at Asia, provided you are not by chance a politician whose sole horizon ends at the tip of your nose, or at best extends only as far as your personal or partisan self-interest.

Within the course of fifty years you will see Asia reborn in the spirit of its ancient Celtic synthesis.

You will see it wisely abstain from all your follies, cautiously free itself of you using your own means, and rebuild around its seven-crowned Sovereign Pontiff the Synarchic Alliance that existed five thousand years ago.

And if, nonetheless persevering in the system of general government based on the Order of Nimrod, you still continue your practice of mutual dismemberment, then you who have closed your ears to the sweet refrains of the Christian promise will be forced to open them to the thundering trumpets of the Last Judgment.

With weapons in hand, Asia will prevent you from coming to disturb its observance of the Law of the Kingdom of God and, with China and Islam in the lead, and under the guidance of your own military instructors, will then arrive to compel your signature at the bottom of the social Promise of the Abramites, of Moses, and of Our Lord Jesus Christ, which you have rejected.

Sooner or later, I believe a thinking Europe will be unable to hesitate between these two perspectives.

In the meantime, I swear an oath for those politicians seeking to carve out a middle course between Anarchy and Synarchy: they will find naught but harmful procrastinations.

As for me, I have finished my labor, and with this book, crowned my three previous *Missions*.

I have done what I had to do, come what may!

To Agartthians and Christians alike, my *Missions* have rationally demonstrated the social and scientific value of the Judeo-Christian promise.

It belongs to all humanity.

It is the luminous cloud that, serving the Son of Man as a pedestal, performs its cyclical return to the sacred mountains from which the Law of the Kingdom of God descended.

Scorn not this Promise, sons of the Magi Kings, Agartthian initiates, and members of the Supreme Council of Brâhatmah.

Fashion yourself as if you were an impregnable fortress surrounded by the thunder and lightning of Sinai and Golgotha.

Come out from the shadow of the Mystery that conceals you from the eyes of Christendom and, with this Promise in hand, return there to claim your civic right and to bless it, your eyes firmly fixed upon the Star that will lead you to Bethlehem.

May I be permitted here to express my wish that my country be the first to receive your visit.

I love my country as you love your own, with all her history, from the ancient Celts of Ram to Vercingetorix, from the hour when Saints John and Mary visited her until the time when Charlemagne placed his valiancy in service to the militant Church, and the sacred moment when Providence itself descended into the soul of Joan of Arc to drive out the invaders.

I love my nation both for her profound poverty and for her dazzling prosperity, both for the crown of Saint Louis that she wears on her head and her hand of justice that breaks this same crown, replacing it with the laurel or oak leaf.

I perceive her to be inspired at all times, whether or not she finds a head, a heart, or an arm for formulating and realizing her thought.

Is she powerful? Generous ideas and sentiments are breathing upon the European Assembly of Nations, and the entire Earth feels them and rejoices. Nations are being formed under her aegis, and they breathe more freely in her spirit.

Is she weakened? The yoke of general government by force is growing heavier, the night of the public anarchy among governments is darkening, and the overburdened nations silently await dismal events.

My nation has broken the chains of captive peoples, beaten down the ignominious gates of the ghettos, and even in the midst of her follies, catching a glimpse of Universality, has felt beating in her heart the soul of the entire Human race.

May she, like ancient Galilee, receive the first visit of the Magi Kings of the new age, and open to them the doors of free passage throughout the entire realm of Judeo-Christianity!

Conclusion

Those faithful to Moses and Jesus will perhaps wonder if there is some degree of incompatibility between their Testaments and the Vedas, between their faith and the arts and sciences of Agarttha.

To this very legitimate concern, I can confidently reply: no, certainly not.

Not only must the universal religious Tradition be reestablished in this way, but also it can only be scientifically verified and justified with the support of the Ramid University. What I am revealing and bringing to Synagogues and Churches alike, as well as to the teaching bodies of all kinds, is an unhoped-for cache of knowledge long held in reserve.

All the wonders introduced to the reader in the previous chapters may well have seemed incredible if not impossible, but I can state in full knowledge of the facts that they represent but a millionth part of the discoveries of all kinds that Agarttha holds in store (on the condition of a treaty guaranteeing its territorial independence) for all the believers and all the sages of the European and American Occident.

The countless treasures reaped from the observations and experiments accumulated by these wise men do not fall only into the two orders of divine and cosmogonic wisdom; they have an equal wealth in the two orders of the human and natural sciences.

During this very century, barely twenty years ago, these sages, with their Sacred Tradition in hand, performed the most extensive geological research of this era, in order to verify the actual limits on this planet of the last Deluge and the possible starting point of its return, some thirteen or fourteen centuries from now. (For more on this see my *Mission of the Jews,* page 159.)

I will perhaps write down one day, if authority is granted me to do so, the history of these amazing explorations, these formidable feats of engineering whereby the Agartthians diverted oceans of sand, causing them to flow into the bowels of the earth, while at the same time continuing to pursue the verification of the sacred traditions for spans of time lasting entire years.

There is also their discovery of a regressed human race with wings and claws, and the no less extraordinary discovery of a species of flying dragon that possesses half-human, half-simian faces. These are but a portion of the concrete facts that these colossal expeditions have discovered, and I would fain extol the glory of their leaders—if I were permitted to reveal their names.

So why then do these sages conceal themselves, why do they not communicate to the Hebrew and Christian religions and universities the countless and inestimable treasures of their divine and cosmic understanding, and of their natural and human knowledge?

It is because the experience of five thousand years has taught them to close their doors to the general government of armed Anarchy, to protect the independence of their territory and the Synarchic structure of their society against all the sectarian and brutal consequences of this anarchy.

But these consequences are nearing their final end, while at the same time the redemptive movement of the Abramites, Moses, and Jesus advances toward its social and cyclical synthesis.

This is the reason why I have no fear of setting European public opinion on the road toward either an alliance with Agarttha, or else toward a formidable explosion of indignation against the governments and religions that would profit from the mystery that envelops Agarttha, in order to strike a blow from the shadows against the independence and social life of this august Ancestor of all the Temples and all the Universities.

Yes, it is there, faithful of Moses, that you shall have the immense happiness of verifying their Egyptian books and all they contain in their hierogrammatic Hebrew text.

Yes, it is there, priests and faithful of Our Lord Jesus Christ, that you shall have the ineffable consolation promised for your fidelity, and shall see all the celestial and social mysteries, sealed within the Hermetic text of your two Testaments, illuminating your consciousness and delighting your hearts.

Yes, it is there, scholars and researchers of all our universities, that you shall find the last word on scientific truth, and—oh! wonders of wonders—you shall read the name of God, such as I described it to you in *Mission of the Jews*, through the quadruple hierarchy of all the sciences and all the arts.

My previous works, and the Synarchic law of History and Human Societies, could only have been based upon a positive and incontestable authority.

And this holy, peaceful, Synarchic authority, which is fifty-five thousand years old, unites Science and Faith, bestows its blessings on all the Religions, all the Universities, and all the Nations, embracing the whole of Heaven and Humanity in one same intelligence and one same love. Ah! Respect it, respect it, and join with me to prevent any attempts made on its life and to give it assurances in the name of all our wisdom, all our science, and our entire civilization, that the woeful experiences of the past will not be repeated.

O priests of all the Christian churches, may you be able to march together on behalf of this temple from religion to religion in the intellectual and social light of the divine Promise of the Gospel, for which my works are naught but the rational commentary!

May you nevermore be lost in futile dogmatic quarrels, and may you thus approach together the scientific verification of our faith. May it be possible to erase from the mind and life of our societies all the sectarian barriers dividing them; and finally, in the name of Christ and Moses, may you restore the intellectual and social peace treaty that was made when man first walked upon the earth, in order to preserve the ancient alliance that I have revealed to you in this *Mission*.

This Church of the Protogonos, known and admired by Moses, Jesus, and the Apostles, far from subtracting something from your holy traditions, will instead restore to you all its hidden Spirit.

I know holy priests who walk on this path of Synarchic Christianity and Universalistic Catholicism.

Among them I would like to name one, who is remarkable as much for his Living Faith as for his knowledge of the social spirit of the Gospels and the Fathers of the Church.

Better inspired than Lamennais,* he remains a Roman Catholic priest; and the untamable spirit of Liberty, Equality, and Fraternity of nations that inflates his lungs with air inhaled from the Holy Scriptures, nonetheless does not hurl him into any political adventure—nor into any personal deviancy.

No, it is from within his own Religion and his own name that His Worship, Canon Roca, who has a degree in letters and is the founder of the Saint Louis School in Perpignan, requests the Synarchic implementation of the social promises made by Christianity.†

This priestly position, on the frontier between civil liberties and the hierarchical discipline of the Church, is as erudite as it is challenging; but it is a definite fact, and it must be said in honor of the papacy, that so far

---

*[Hughes-Félicité Robert de Lamennais (1782–1854), a priest whose liberal leanings were condemned by Pope Gregory XVI in the encyclical *Mirani vos,* which eventually led to his leaving the church. His views could be seen as a precursor to liberation theology. —*Trans.*]

†*La Crise fatale et le Salut de l'Europe, étude critique sur les Missions de M. de Saint-Yves* [The Fatal Crisis and Salvation of Europe, a Critical Study of the Missions of Saint-Yves], Paris: Garnier 1885. *La Fin de l'Ancien Monde* [The End of the Ancient World], Paris: Calmann Lévy, 1886.

no finger-pointing or blame has come to halt the voluntary mission of the saintly and valiant priest to whom I am paying homage here.

May this individual permit me to put one of my wishes into words.

May he strive to gather a group of priests from his church, and may they go together to ask the Pope personally for authorization and the right to exist as an *Order* in this current of Synarchic ideas.

An immense step will have been made toward social salvation, not only for our country but also for the whole of Christendom, once such a consecration has been granted.

To the best of my knowledge, Abbé Roca has rejected, on two separate occasions, the miter that was offered to him, as he believes he can more usefully serve his faith, his parish, and his country by remaining free.

An *Order* of priests demonstrating such self-sacrifice and such good will, authorized by Rome and accepted in advance by the French Government, would have an incalculable impact upon the solution of the difficult problem of the Synarchic reconciliation of the two ecclesiastic and civil societies.

Furthermore, all of this is naught but a wish, as every believer is free to make, and its usefulness should be assessed only by a competent authority.

My works, as I have said elsewhere, are primarily addressed to the Gentiles, and to the educated who have received instruction from our Universities as well as from the mundane literature of the advanced studies, and who no longer know upon what fixed point of certainty to focus their eclecticism, whether it be in philosophy, exegesis, history, comparative theology, in the presence of facts revealed by the natural sciences, or finally in matters concerning the conditions of the social order in the present anarchy of doctrines, parties, and classes.

It is within this category of mental attitudes, which extends from our students to our scholars, from our thinkers and sociologists to the most enlightened members of our high society or ruling class, that I am carrying out my intellectual movement.

With them, I reason and display to the best of my ability the validity of the Synarchic Law and the universal concordance of the truths and realities that form the total object of Knowledge.

The majority of these minds will remain attached for worldly reasons to the formalism of our religious practices.

The majority desire that these practices be maintained, dreading their reversal through revolution, even while appearing to be more or less detached intellectually from them.

My works show them that Judeo-Christianity has had, and preserves in a latent state, reserves of social action that are more formidable than has been suspected by rationalists since Montesquieu, by Encyclopedists until Fabre d'Olivet, and finally by contemporary exegetes.

As for the intellectual stock held by the Hebrew texts of Judeo-Christianity, they can only gain in value by being further studied, scientifically and consciously.

But it is necessary to take all the esotericism of the natural, human, cosmogonic, and divine sciences not from authors of debatable merit, but from the Universities where they are preserved in all their authenticity. Among these universities, Agarttha is the most important.

I will now move on to look at that which concerns not only the cognizable Mysteries contained within the Hebrew text of our two Testaments, but also the Hellenic synthesis crafted by the Fathers of the Universal Church, namely the transfiguration of ancient Israel and its entire secret doctrine.

Here again, despite the many and often intentional veils placed upon it, its conformity with the spirit of the ancient Ramid Cycles, and its concordance with the past and present University of the Church of the Protogonos and the pre-Abramite Iswara-El, are visible and demonstrable and authorize an alliance of the universities with Agarttha.

In fact, the synthetic task achieved in Alexandria under the invisible breath of the spirit of Christ was in no way a banal work, nor was it a work that could be undertaken in any era without the support of initiates of the highest degree—even if, under the eye and hand of Latin Caesarism, the Epopts who presided, visibly or not, over this synthetic work had to mask esotericism beneath exotericism, and Israelite Christianity under Hellenic Christianity.

The ancient astronomical genethliac has served as a cyclical sphere for this hermetically sealed intellectual ark; and there is not a temple or a sanctuary in existence that has not been made a part of this edifice of the new covenant by some initiate who has brought into it, at the very least, the nomenclature of the sacraments, symbols, rites, and mysteries involved in so many occult sciences and hidden truths.

It is in this way that the Hellenic-Christian synthesis contains within itself—nominally or really—all the degrees corresponding to the initiation of the ancient Ramid Universities of Paradesa, Chaldea, Egypt, Thrace, Ramid Celtia, and Etruria.

It is for this reason that Saint Paul in his Agartthian epistles told the Romans that they had already known the Law.

Furthermore, throughout the whole of Antiquity, the Law signified the Science of natural, human, and divine things.

In our churches and even in the order of the primary teachings themselves, the nomenclature of the objects of this ancient Knowledge survives in its totality, even in the theurgy of our religion.

The cosmic festivals are in their exact places within their respective astronomical seasons.

The Worship of the Ancestors and that of the Generations have their true symbols and sacraments.

With regard to the Mysteries of what lies beyond death, their triple religion is judiciously observed.

The Day of the Dead authorizes the wise and conscious worship of souls; All Saint's Day authorizes that of the glorified Spirits.

The worship of Angels, which, along with prayer, is one of the foundations of Divine Magic, is also as legitimate in our own churches as it is in Agarttha, under the name of the cyclical or cosmic spirits who we designate by the titles of Angels, Archangels, Principalities, Powers, Virtues, Dominations, Thrones, Cherubim, and Seraphim.

In this nomenclature we have preserved intact the nominal disposition of the Cosmic Mysteries: not only as they were envisioned by the Judeo-Christian Kabbalists, not only as they are practiced in secret by the current disciples of Saint John the Baptist and certain esoteric schools in Cairo, Sinai, and Arabia, but also as they are professed scientifically and practically by the Magi of Agarttha.

Finally, so as to leave no doubt about the nature of their antisectarian and Kabbalistic work, the first Christian initiates stamped the three synoptic Gospels and that of Saint John with the quadruple seal of the most secret of the sciences contained within the Kabbalah of Moses and the Prophets: the Angel, the Eagle, the Bull, and the Lion.

Outside to the Hellenic current itself, the writers of the Hebrew texts of the gospels sealed within them all the clues that make it possible to see their connection with the Israelite synthesis carried out earlier in the Temples of Babylon by Daniel, an Agartthian initiate and Sovereign Pontiff of the Chaldeans, as well as their connection with the most secret part of the Jewish Kabbalah, known under the name of P.R.D.S., Paradesa: see *Mission of the Jews,* page 655.

This significant hierogram was sometimes replaced among the first Christian initiates by the name of *Glorious Christ.*

The Apocalypse of Saint John was written under the head of the twenty-two Mysteries of the ancient synthesis, and its fifty-six complementary hieroglyphs.

Finally, it is not until the openings of the Epistles that the Hebrew Text shows all the letters of the name of Agarttha: אגרת אל אפסים, אגרת אל רומים, אגרת אל גלטים, *Agarttha-al-Ephesim, Agarttha-al-Galatim, Agarttha-al-Romim,* Agarttha to the Ephesians, Agarttha to the Galatians, Agarttha to the Romans.

The Christian Cycle, being the supreme fruition of the movement of the Abramites and Moses, therefore positively has as its goal the universal renewal of the Ramid Synarchy, just as I have shown in *Mission of the Jews*.

Likewise, the people of the Abramite, Mosaic, and Christian covenant, including the Talmudist movement of Muhammad, possess in their synthesis—in a nominal or real state—what the Ramid Universe still preserves today in a state that is not only of the sciences but of the experimental arts.

In the hieratic text of Moses, the principles of the quadruple hierarchy of knowledge are preserved and summarily exposed in their progressions, beneath the triply ciphered hierograms.

In Agarttha, each of these Principles is the subject of numerous volumes of analysis, based on experiments beyond number.

But Europeans should not regard those texts that have entered into their possession via the school of Calcutta as the true Sanskrit and Vedic texts.

For more than three centuries now, due to political circumstances, the sacred texts, everywhere but in Agarttha, have been systematically distorted. For more on this subject, you may refer to an extremely rare tome, printed in India through the pains taken by the Brahman Reform Party, entitled *Report of the Maharaj Libel Case and of the Bhattin Conspiracy Case Connected with It,* Bombay, 1862.

Finally, it is in Agarttha alone that the linguistics of which Saint John speaks at the opening of his Gospel have been practiced for some five hundred and fifty-six centuries without interruption, in order that this incontestable academic authority may unreservedly give, to whomever it chooses, all the lost secrets from the Hebrew-Egyptian text of our own holy scriptures and the positive keys to their mysteries.

Concerning the value of these keys as well as the exceptional expertise of the Agartthian scholars, I can invoke if necessary—in Palestine—the information provided by the venerable Gaonim and Kabbalim of Jerusalem.

I could also invoke—in Arabia—that of the respectable Imams and Mufti scholars of Mecca and Medina.

I have reason to believe that these pious figures do in fact know to what extent their foundations rest upon the exegetic and magical science of the high initiates of Agarttha.

I am only citing these facts and these names to indicate a providential coincidence that is quite remarkable.

In the East, it is precisely the leaders of the religions that appear to be the least open to any kind of alliance who are the first to be affected by the luminous spirit of their common Promise, and inclined by it to renewal of the Ancient Covenant and Synarchy.

It is thus in error that superficial criticism accuses these religious leaders of systematic and social impotence, immobility, and ignorance, for which politics alone would be the cause.

Like all our European sovereigns, they are more or less the prisoners of war of the infernal politics that my works have unmasked throughout all time.

Without lifting any more than necessary the veil covering the divine action toward universal Synarchy, I can permit myself to point out this fact, which is of the utmost importance, to the leaders of our different Churches: there is no longer any sectarianism in the leadership of the main religions of the East.

Finally, with regard to Christian esotericism, I will only add a word to demonstrate its reality, and this word I will borrow from the divine lips of Our Lord Jesus Christ: His disciples came to him asking why he spoke to the people in parables.

And he answered them saying:

"You have been given the ability to know the Secrets of the Kingdom of Heaven; this has not been given to them. This is why I speak to them in parables."

These all-important words are found in Saint Matthew, chapter thirteen, verses 10, 11, and 13. They incontestably prove existence of the esoteric doctrine Jesus was preaching in the synagogues under the name of the Gospel of the Kingdom, which the Kabbalists knew under the name of Paradesa, and which finally the initiates of the early Christian centuries would contemplate under the name of Glorious Christ.

The Christianity of the crucifixion is the veil that hides the Christianity of the glorification.

Elsewhere, Christ again speaks to us saying:

"Ask and it shall be given, Seek and you shall find, knock and the door shall be opened to you."

These words are found in Saint Luke, chapter 11, verse 9; and they prove that Our Lord Jesus Christ, like Moses, knew beyond any possibility of doubt that Humanity itself held a reserve treasure in a sealed Tabernacle, at whose door one could knock, ask, and receive. For more on this see my *Mission of the Jews,* page 7.

I have only cited the preceding words to show, out of the very mouth of the Savior, the affirmation of the esoteric science, the certitude that the Mysteries of the Kingdom of God are cognizable, and that finally, knowledge of this is guarded in a very secure location on this very Earth.

Here, the reader who has followed me through all my *Missions* will now be definitely and more than abundantly convinced of the true nature of all the facts gathered therein, as well as of all the proofs these same facts positively scream concerning the intellectual and social constitution of the World of Antiquity.

Finally, the divine plan of the History of Human Societies will have clearly appeared to all conscientious and sufficiently educated readers, not as a metaphysical system but as an objective truth and reality, for which past and existing facts provide incontestable proof.

Agarttha is the static center from which radiated the ancient

Universal Synarchy of the Lamb and Aries, and from which began the Renewal of this Law of the Kingdom of God through the Abramites, who served as an intermediary.

Finally, the orthodox Egyptian colleges to which Moses and Jethro belonged were stirred by the same spirit that Our Lord Jesus Christ, after the disappearance of Mosaic Israel, breathed anew into the soul of the whole of Humanity and into the whole of the eternal Israel.

All the social dynamism of the Abramite, Mosaic, and Christian movement is still proven and undeniably verified today by this static center of the original Synarchy, which remains unchanged even at the time I am writing these lines.

Such is the Unity and the Universality of the General Government of God, in course of being renewed through and despite the general government of Satan, the Antigod, and the Antichrist, by which I mean the governmental system inaugurated in Babylon five thousand years ago, which my *Missions* have followed step by step through the entire span of Universal History, unmasking all its characteristics and all its consequences.

Works of this nature, if written in Asia by an Asian native, would have already gathered together millions of men of science and conscience ready to take peaceful action toward the definitive reorganization of the Planet.

In Europe, people will probably confine themselves to asking me for proof of my proof, and will cast doubt on the very existence of Agarttha, telling me: "Once there was a city named Agarttha, is this the same as the holy land of which you are speaking?"

"If it is the same, then what you are saying does not add up; if it is not at all the same, can you give us the means to verify the existence of this Synarchic University that you have revealed?"

I would like nothing better that to provide this proof of the proof.

However, until a treaty has been signed by Europe that guarantees the continued independence of Agarttha, one will easily understand my reservations in doing so.

And I add that even if I were compelled by a sovereign, any sovereign at all, to come and tell him more on this subject, it would be impossible for me to respond to this request without previously having in hand the European guarantee of which I am speaking.

I should nevertheless make an exception for the leader of my own country, and I will express in advance that it would be my honor to reveal more on this subject to him if he should deem it appropriate to summon me.

Alone in his company, I will unequivocally tell him the steps necessary to put in an official request to Agarttha on behalf of those laureates or professors of our advanced studies who may desire to go there to see firsthand the sciences and arts that are taught in the Synarchic University of Aries, so that they may be accepted for initiation.

It will be our own scholars who, once they have been initiated, will say on their return—to the extent they believe themselves capable of so doing—whether or not this university metropolis exists; whether or not the sciences and arts about which I have spoken are truly embraced and practiced there; and whether the esotericism of all the holy books of the world is merely a joke, an invention of the Kabbalists of the Middle Ages, or a formidable reality that involves the four hierarchies of total Knowledge.

It will be easy to understand why, in a subject so unknown as this, as I said earlier, for diplomats and missionaries alike, any other kind of verification of my proof would be inadmissible; because, truth be told, it would be too easy to set up in opposition to me the self-interested denial of any agent of some given sect or political party, whether it be European or any other.

Lastly, in addition to the verification I am proposing, there is yet one more, but one that does not depend upon me. This would be the presence, in Paris itself, of an Agartthian embassy.

One final word: I have often been criticized for having signed my *Mission of the Sovereigns* with the name of one of these rulers.

Not only did I do this, but I still fully support my decision to do so, and my peremptory reasons are as follows.

Here I can hear the cries of indignation of the courtiers, the worldly, and the flatterers of all who hold power.

What's this! they will say, it is not enough that you have directly addressed in the present book two Sovereign Pontiffs, a Queen, and an Emperor, but here we find this writer pushing his impudence even farther into sovereignty itself.

They would of course be right, if my conception of sovereign duties were the same as theirs: the ultimate goal of every form of ambition, covetousness, and vanity.

I can even hear the same voices shouting: *He really believes this has happened.*

Yes, I do believe it, but not as it is understood by the wasps of republican or monarchical authority, the political atheists, or the social materialists.

They undoubtedly do not know that not only in the Synarchic structure of the Cycle of Ram, but also in Christian esotericism, to rule is to serve, *regnare servire est.*

This was in fact the nature of the Synarchic kingdoms, which, for the last five thousand years, have not reigned in this world.

It is also by virtue of this that all initiates were and still are kings, and as such, by right if not by fact, they were and still are part of the Council of those who claim the leadership of nations.

Among the Romans themselves who, as Saint Paul told them, had known the law through Numa but had never observed it, the emperors, while pursuing their wars of Neo-Babylonian anarchism against the universities of the Synarchy of Antiquity, nevertheless affected a respectful deference toward certain initiates.

This is still the way Rajahs today act toward the Epopts of Agarttha.

Only the sovereigns of the Middle Ages and the Renaissance, in their parody of the ancient Royal Art, did not allow truth to speak to them freely, but rather, alas! with its face fully revealed, yet behind the figure of some self-styled lunatic, such as Triboulet or Rabelais.

The times have passed, fortunately, in which the Wisdom of Antiquity had to conceal itself beneath the mask of madness; but the times have returned—Praise be to God on high!—in which the direct Logos can and must awaken again to action and speak to the powers of the Earth, provided it can find a missionary with a heart humble enough to address kings as equals.

Indeed, only the most profound humility is inaccessible to the bedazzlement of what we call the grandeurs of this world below.

The proud do not speak to kings in this way; they flatter them in order to make use of them, or else insult them in order to glorify themselves.

With respect to myself, political powers, whether republican or monarchist, will never have heard either in my works or in my discourse anything but the Eternal law and the religious wish to see their own salvation.

In this final *Mission,* I am showing them the enduring power of Synarchic institutions composed of three social powers:

1. Teaching authority based on the Order of God
2. Power of Justice based on the Order of Melchizedek
3. Local economic power based on the Order of the Ancients

This enduring power, with respect to Agarttha, has already lasted some fifty-five thousand six hundred and forty-seven years.

Finally, like Christopher Columbus coming to kings and begging them to allow him to give them a world, I am bringing them one even larger, not only as measured in space but in spirit; and I beseech the European powers to respect this ancient New World, I again charitably warn them of all the dangers of all kinds that they will encounter if they attack this world with violence, and I again stress the absolute necessity of an Alliance founded on Synarchy.

Finally, I would like to bring this *Mission* to a close with the expression of a wish. I long to see the coming of the day when a European ecumenical council shall take place, in which all the religions are represented, as well as all the Universities, all the Lodges of the thirty-third degree, and all the sovereign leaders of our European nations. And I long myself to be invited to attend this council, in order to present and defend the Synarchic law of History and Human Societies, assisted by two Magi from Agarttha!

Epilogue

I am going to show the majority of my readers that I am no less aware of what takes place in their thought as I am of what is happening in the crypts of Agarttha.

In fact, everyone, with a few very rare exceptions, will say or think the following:

> This man is a lunatic, or else the victim or the originator of a hoax. In any case, he is quite naïve if he imagines that the Pope and the Sovereigns whom he addresses as an equal, in an intolerably apocalyptic tone, are going to take him seriously.
>
> The president of Republic will clearly refrain from incurring the ridicule that would result from inviting him to visit and thus accepting publicly that this book might be anything other than a cock and bull story.

But that is not all; for if some readers who are better informed about the sciences and secrets of India have the courage to raise their voices and say that I am not a madman, nor the victim or creator of a hoax, then we shall hear other allegations in a torrent of sarcasms upon sarcasms, insults upon insults, and calumnies upon calumnies.

I know in advance who will speak, and even better who will make others speak.

Why should this be cause for surprise?

What man has ever brought Humanity a handful of truths without being repaid with many more persecutions than those that have fallen upon *Mission of the Jews* and will continue their song and dance still more loudly against this *Mission of India*?

So, far from complaining, I say in advance to my friends: Have courage; and to my enemies: Thank You.

APPENDICES

Portrait of "the other Easterner" (sent by M.L.J.)

"The other Easterner" in the company of merchants

ای این عکس ووه برنرست کمی تا مرگیی شفید
دوخطه شده، این بادار بن بح قع میدارد

Inscription on the back of the photograph, with its translation:
This photo depicts the late Prince, who was photographed with
me and a Kashmir merchant.

Hardjji Scharipf

[Translation]

<u>Saint Yves d'Alveydre</u>

The Mission of India in Europe

The only copy of this work that escaped the total destruction of the first edition decided upon by the author following threats coming from India.

This copy belonged to the late Marquis of Saint Yves and was given to Dr. Encausse [Papus] by Count Keller.

This copy was reproduced when the work was published by Dorbon.

Oct. 1910

Papus

Letter from the esotericist Papus (Dr. Gérard Encausse) found in the sole surviving copy of the first edition of Mission de l'Inde used for reprinting, explaining that the author had ordered the book destroyed.

NOTICE

It is with true emotion that we publish today this previously unknown work by our venerated teacher, the Marquis of Saint-Yves d'Alveydre.

Mission of the Jews, a truly luminous key to Universal History, and *Mission of the Sovereigns,* a truly miraculous clarification of the secret machinery of the European nations, are the work of a seeker provided with only intellectual keys.

The present book is the result of a twofold series of researches that are intellectual at first, then astral.

This is the first work by Saint-Yves in which practical experiments in out of body traveling have allowed the author to enter the most secret sanctuaries of the Earth in order to verify their oral teachings.

The structure of Agarttha is revealed for the first time to Western readers, and the question of the one (not the many) Mahatma is restored to its true place.

It is not without an ineffable smile that the Initiates of the Brahmanic Church hear Europeans who have attempted to study Buddhism speak of the "Mahatmas." After multiplying their number, they have been made into a "College." In America, diplomas have even been issued from an alleged College of Mahatmas! Saint-Yves, in an appendix to his book, *Joan of Arc Victorious,* published a short note on this topic. The title of Mahatma belongs to the Brahmanic Church and it characterizes the duties of a single individual. There are no more colleges of Mahatmas than there are Councils of Lutheran Cardinals. The future will show decisive evidence that the springs from which Saint-Yves drank are not only real, but still alive.

But these are sacred matters. Polemic would be out of place here, and our Teacher never responded to the vile insults cast against his work and his person.

Here, we cannot forget also to thank Count Alexandre Keller, who has been so kind as to send us the sole existing copy of this valuable work, which was destined to not see the light of day during our Teacher's lifetime.

We respectfully commend the reading of these pages to those "who wish to know."

The Friends of Saint-Yves
February 13, 1910

APPENDIX
February 13, 1910

In order to shed some light upon the noble physiognomy of Prince Hardjij [*sic*] Scharipf, who following the publication of *Mission of the Jews* spontaneously came to France for the impartial purpose of initiating Saint-Yves d'Alveydre into the knowledge of Sanskrit—and also in order to avoid any hesitant remarks concerning the individual whose features we were happy to reproduce faithfully in this volume with the authorization of Saint-Yves' family—we publish below the text of two letters: one addressed by the Prince to the author of the *Missions,* the other addressed to the Prince by General Dumont.

3rd Army Corps General of the Division
Office: No. 7 Commander of the Army Corps
Paris, January 8, 1886

From General Dumont, Commander of the Third Army Corps, to Milord Hardjij [*sic*] Scharipf, Brahman-Guru-Pandit.

Milord, I am quite touched by the affectionate memory that you clearly wish to keep of me and by the delicate way in which you expressed it, on the occasion of the new year.

Everything that your former and current students tell me proves that I was the instrument of Providence by putting you in contact with our dear Marquis of Saint-Yves, and with the angel who inspired and sustained him so well.

It seems that the time has come to join East and West together under the common domain of science, and no one is more capable than you and your worthy students of leading such an immense undertaking to a successful conclusion, one that could be so fertile with results for the good of humanity.

May Brahma and the God of the Christians, who differ only in name—or may I say the Master of the Universe—second you in the fulfillment of your holy task. This is the wish that I send you from the bottom of my heart.

As for me, I will always be happy and proud of having been able to contribute to bringing together three souls so well made to understand one another and so worthy of the high mission entrusted to them.

If it please, Milord, with the homage of my deepest respect.
(Signed) General F. Dumont

Facsimile of the letter from the Prince to Saint-Yves d'Alveydre

[Translation]

From no. 108, Rue de Cormeille, in Levallois-Perret,
this 24th of December [18]87

To His Excellency Monsieur the Marquis of Saint-Yves d'Alveydre
in his hotel, 27 Rue Vernet, Paris

Monsieur the Marquis,

May you deign to permit that, among the crowds who today will be rendering unto you the homage of their blessings for Noël (the happy & merry Xmas) and their wishes for the new year about to begin: that I as well (your humble [Sanskrit]) may also have access to you in order to bear witness to the sentiments of my profound respect, and to wish you all the good things that my respectful heart can and must call upon you.

May each one of your desires be instantaneously satisfied! may all that you hope for be crowned with the happiest success! may all your projects have a satisfying result in keeping with the ineffable qualities of your benevolent and generous heart! May the most flowering praises and the purest joy forever embellish your life and that of Madame the Marquise, your beloved and noble wife! May recognition from such a great number of persons (including my own family), and your beautiful soul ceaselessly filled with kindness, recompense you at least in part for your solicitude for the good of all people!

May the benedictions of Brahma-Dévam, called upon you for these good reasons, Monsieur the Marquis, as well as upon your holy wife of such happy renown, be scattered upon you unceasingly, amen, and if the justice of men has not the balance needed to see the full extent of your so distinguished and multiple merits, nor the means of rewarding them worthily here below: then may the satisfaction felt by a generous heart, seeking to contribute to the good of its fellows, Yes, may this satisfaction compensate for it.

And by the grace of our Samraj in particular, allow me to continue (during my brief sojourn) to receive your valuable protection and your flattering benevolence, and in order to prove it, may you deign to accept the homage of the respect and devotion with which I declare myself:

Monsieur the Marquis of Saint-Yves,
Your very devoted and humble Brahm,
Hardjji Scharipf Bagwandas
(born in Bombay, the 25th of December 1838)

P.S. Pardon me for informing you that your command and desire were executed (a long time) after your visit of the 2nd of last November, but all this will be reviewed and explained upon your next visit (God willing).

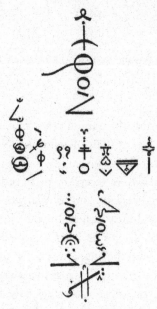

Dedication to the Sovereign Pontiff

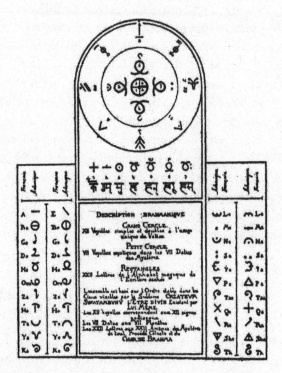

"Watan" alphabet published in L'Archéomètre.

EXTRACT FROM *JEANNE D'ARC VICTORIEUSE*
["JOAN OF ARC VICTORIOUS"] (PARIS: L. SAUVAITRE, 1890):
TWENTY-FIFTH CANTO (PAGE 283)

"Look!" says the Archangel.—She looked back.
The People of the Divine Spirits illuminated
            The Seven Times Holy Prophetess
The Cathedral was set aglow by this; and yet
The Priests crossing through believed themselves alone, groping
            Along their dark path within this Enclosure.

"Hosanna!" said the Archangel; and the Church struck up
On the Organ and the Harp a Divine Hosanna
            Heard by a single Soul,
The one that Michael in his Immortal Arms
Carried palpitating to the foot of the High Altar,
            That enveloped His Flight with Flame.

Behind it, the Invisible World shimmered:
The Triumphant Church, Here Below, sent
            For some sublime Mystery,
One and Triple, Three Leaders, Three Choirs into the Unprecedented.
One of the Himalayas, the Other of Sinai,
            *And the third of Solyme.**

The Eldest One bore the Vedas: this was Ram,
Heir to Noah, testator of Abraham.
            His Tiara had Seven Crowns.
Seven Rishis, like Him veiled in diamonds,
Accompanied him, dragging with them from Heaven the gleams
            Of the Thrones and Principalities.

Crosses in hand, by the side of their white Brahatma
The Mahanga soared with the Mahatma
            Beneath the Vatanic Tiara,
Orienting the Seven, Stars of the Vedas,
Then, Miter in their Brows, Three Hundred and Sixty Bagwandas,
            Zodiac of the Brahmanic Heaven.

---

*[The biblical name for Jerusalem. —*Trans.*]

And from the Himalayas, who in the Heavens sang
The Ancient Synarchy and its holy Agarttha,
          Irradiating all these Arks,
Gazing upon Joan through all their dazzled Saints
Praying her to one day be reborn for the Land
          Of the Church of the Patriarchs.

Ram embraced the Altar.—Another Gleam
Soared from Sinai. Raising the Testament
          Of the Hebraic Synarchy,
Moses of the Golden Horns illuminated His People;
Triple Counsel of God, the Angels, the elders,
          The entire Mosaic Church.

And all, joining their hands, looked toward Joan,
Praying for their Sheep of East and West,
          Of North and South, and everywhere dying,
So that she might one day return for the Hebrews,
Raising her Angelic Standard above them,
          Gathering back together all their lost Tribes.

Moses, having kissed the palpitating Altar,
Other Glories suddenly glowed from Golgotha,
          Setting fire to the Basilica:
It was Saint Peter with the Second Testament,
Dazzling from afar with His Radiance
          The entire Evangelical Church.

The Apostle, by embracing the Altar, illuminated it;
Between Moses and Ram, Triple Glory, He soared.
          The Gospel combined its Flames
With the Rays of the Sepher and the Vedas, so strongly
That the Logos cracked open with a supreme effort
          Its Tabernacle over these Souls.

By itself, the Holy of Holies let ascend
Its pure gold Chalice, which floated straight to
          The Apostle and beneath a Host;
And the Three Heads of the Church with their Testaments,

Prostrate, heard in the flaring up of its Flames
  The word of the Eucharist:

"Prepare the Crown and the Palm Leaf, all Three!
I coronate Joan of Arc daughter of the King of Kings
  Upon the work she realizes,
Simultaneously confirming Three Revelations,
My Threefold Law given to the Nations through you,
  My Promise to my Threefold Church!"

"I need a Chosen People of the Holy Ghost:
France! It is still you, with whom Joan of Heaven fell in love,
  You that her Miracle designated!
Be the Standard Bearer of My Divine Rule,
And the sons of Nimrod will devastate you in vain:
  You will defeat them under this Sign!"

"Go, all repeat to My Threefold Israel
That I am its True Eternal Christ, King of Heaven,
  As was proven by My Maid!
Yes, France! She saved the world by saving you,
By unfurling over All, Flag of the Living God,
  The Universal Synarchy!"

Note:

The Mother Church of non-sectarian Brahmanism is still structured as it was presented here for the first time to Europeans.

The Synarchic Trinity is represented there by the Sovereign Pontiff or *Brahatma,* Leader of the Teaching Order, and his Two Assessors, the *Mahatma,* Head of the Judicial Order, and the *Mahanga,* head of the economic order. The seven *Rishis* and the three hundred and sixty *Bagwandas* or Cardinals together all form the great college of the Sacerdotal University that reproduces in its organization the entire pre-diluvium Synthesis of Antiquity, based upon the System of the Word of which Saint John speaks.

As a consequence of the Revolutions that sundered the ancient Synarchic organization revealed in *Mission of the Jews,* this Mother University has increasingly kept her Mysteries sealed. Her mystical name, Agarttha,

Ungraspable by Violence, makes it quite clear that she conceals her place of residence from the curious.

Joan of Arc Victorious will be read there, as will *Mission of the Jews*.

May the Patriarchal Church, the Mosaic Church, and the Church of the Gospels be united in a shared glorification of the Daughter of God and her Synarchic Standard!

INDEX